Women have an amazir

When our children do messy things, no matter how old
they are, it is our nature to try to clean up after them and
to make everything all right again. When we can't, the
despair is great and the desperation is all pervasive. Cathy
Blount has waded through the mess and has come out on
the other side a new and renewed woman, despite the fact
her precious son's messy choices have left her totally helpless. She has found that Jesus alone is the Redeemer of our
messes, and He alone can be trusted.

If you are a mother, a son, a husband, a daughter, or a
dad, Cathy's firsthand account of walking through the valley of homosexuality will give you a perspective that every
Christian needs to consider.

Jan Silvious,
Author of *Foolproofing Your Life*
& Big Girls Don't Whine

There's No Place Like *Home*

There's No Place Like Home

How I Found My Way Back

Cathy Blount

TATE PUBLISHING & Enterprises

Published by Tate Publishing & Enterprises, LLC
127 E. Trade Center Terrace | Mustang, Oklahoma 73064 USA
1.888.361.9473 | www.tatepublishing.com

Tate Publishing is committed to excellence in the publishing industry. The company reflects the philosophy established by the founders, based on Psalm 68:11,
"The Lord gave the word and great was the company of those who published it."

Book design copyright © 2008 by Tate Publishing, LLC. All rights reserved.
Cover design by Nathan Harmony
Interior design by Lynly D. Taylor

Published in the United States of America

ISBN: 978-1-60604-594-7
1. Christian Living: Relationships: Sexuality
2. Christian Living: Grief, Suffering, and Consolation
08.10.13

Dedication

This book is lovingly dedicated to the memory of Barbara Johnson. Because of her message of hope and healing in the book *Where Does a Mother Go to Resign?*, I have hope for restoration and healing for my son. May her legacy live on.

Note to the Reader

Names have been changed. Where those names are changed, an asterisk will appear.

Also, the information for this book was influenced by:

The Wizard of Oz: copyright 1939, Supplementary Material Compilation copyright 2005, Turner Entertainment Co. Distributed by Warner Home Video, Inc. 4000 Warner Blvd, Burbank, California 91522

And on *Miracle on 34th Street*: 1947 Twentieth Century Fox Film Corporation, copyright renewed 1974 by Twentieth Century Fox Film Corporation. Twentieth Century Fox Home Entertainment, Inc. P.O. Box 900, Beverly Hills, California 90213–0900

Love Won Out is a registered trademark of Focus on the Family, copyright 2008 *www.lovewonout.com*

Table of Contents

The Storm

Poor Dorothy. Mean old Miss Gulch saw Toto chasing her cat again and digging in her garden. She was so angry that she proceeded to hit poor Toto with a rake! He wasn't really bad; he was just doing what dogs do. Afraid of what Miss Meany might do next, Dorothy and Toto ran as fast as they could to the farm to tell Aunt Em and Uncle Henry what had happened, but they were too busy counting the chickens to listen. Dorothy tried to tell the three farm hands about her dilemma, but Zeke was too busy getting the hogs in, Hunk was at work on the wagon and didn't have time to listen, and Hickory was tinkering with "the contraption" and had no time for childish stories. After fretting for a bit, Dorothy relaxed somewhat and convinced herself that since there was no sign of Miss Gulch coming up the road, the worst was over. But the worst was yet to come.

By and by, Miss Meany arrived at the farm to speak to Aunt Em and Uncle Henry; she said the dog was a menace to the neighborhood, (she was a fine one to be talking since she was the meanest person around for miles), and the sheriff had sent an order with her to seize Toto.

"He didn't mean it! Please don't let her take him!" Dorothy cried. Amid sobs, wails, and a torrent of tears, the sad, grief-stricken little girl cried and begged Auntie Em and Uncle Henry to do something to stop her, but they could not disobey the law. Poor Dorothy held little Toto in her arms as long as she could but finally had to surrender her beloved pet. Unable to bear the pain, she ran to her room, flung herself on the bed, and cried her eyes out.

After handing Toto over to Miss Gulch, Auntie Em said she would like to tell her a thing or two but couldn't because she was a Christian woman and promptly ran to her room to cry too. Uncle Henry was left to handle the transaction of Toto. Miss Meany had brought along a basket with a lid, and the little dog was placed inside. Uncle Henry looked like he might cry any moment but managed to refrain. Feeling satisfied with herself, Miss Gulch marched out to her bicycle and strapped the basket securely behind her seat. I guess Miss Gulch hadn't heard that pride goes before a fall, but she was about to experience the truth of the Word. Riding away, clever Toto pushed the lid open with his nose and quietly jumped to freedom! Old Gulch kept pedaling along, impressed with her accomplishment, unaware of how silly she would look when she arrived at the sheriff's office!

Little Toto raced back home and jumped through Dorothy's window to her bed where she lay weeping. Surprised and relieved to see Toto, Dorothy decided the only thing to do was run away. Once Miss Gulch realized the dog had escaped, she would be back and next time possibly bring reinforcements. If leaving home would save Toto's life, it was what she must do.

Shoving a few things into her suitcase, she hurriedly placed Auntie Em's photo into her small basket, the place she kept the things closest to her heart, climbed out the window, and fled without even looking back. Dorothy must have felt terribly sad as she thought about what she would do and where she would go. After all, she was only a little girl. She certainly couldn't go back home—she would lose

Toto. Dorothy sadly trudged along in deep thought. How she loved Aunt Em and Uncle Henry. How would she ever bear being away from them?

Looking up from her downcast gaze, she noticed a wagon with the name *Professor Marvel* painted on its side. She read the smaller print and discovered that the professor traveled around to meet important people like kings and such and see the wonders of the world. Somewhat encouraged, the idea came to her that maybe she and Toto could join the professor and see the world. Hellos were exchanged and after asking Professor Marvel if she and her little dog might indeed join him in his travels, the wise professor insisted he consult the crystal ball first before making a decision. Having lived many years on this earth and seeing many things, he sensed some unrest in Dorothy. Was she running away? It didn't take a rocket scientist to figure that one out. A young girl with her dog and suitcase was an instant giveaway.

After instructing her to close her eyes and surrender her small basket, the place she kept the things closest to her heart, where Aunt Em's picture was, he carefully and quietly looked inside. Finding the photo and making note of the woman's appearance so he could use it when he looked into the crystal ball, he gave her permission to open her eyes. What a sad tale he told! The professor said a woman was crying, and not only that, she was holding her chest. Was this somebody Dorothy knew? Of course it was! It was none other than Aunt Em. Dorothy's heart felt like it would break in two. She became terribly upset and worried by this news and knew what she must do. She must go home.

But a storm was brewing on the horizon. Clouds

began churning round and round. The wind blew so hard it almost knocked poor Dorothy down. The sky grew dark and threatening. Would she make it back home? She had to! Oh, poor Auntie Em!

If only she hadn't run away, she might have been safely squirreled away in the storm shelter bundled up in Auntie Em's soft, comforting arms. Why did she run away? It was a terrible mistake, and now she might not make it home to safety. With Toto tucked under her arm, she lumbered along against the wind.

Back home, the farmhands, Aunt Em, and Uncle Henry looked for Dorothy and called out her name. Auntie Em's worried face and quivering lips revealed the fear that lay deep within her as she shouted into the boisterous wind, "Dorothy, Dorothy! Where are you, Dorothy?"

But Dorothy couldn't hear them calling; all she could hear was the fierce wind. How could a storm come up so quickly? Perhaps Dorothy ignored the early warning signs, a warm summer breeze that somehow worked itself into a strong wind, a darkening sky that was filled with sunshine only minutes before. It seemed almost like the clouds quietly gathered together and whispered their plan of destruction while no one noticed, until it was upon them.

Upon reaching home, the storm grew stronger by the minute, and poor Dorothy could barely stand as she struggled her way into the house, calling out and searching for Auntie Em. The curtains flapped wildly, and the front door banged loudly against the house until it was torn off the hinges and tossed aside.

"Auntie Em, Auntie Em, where are you?" *The storm shelter-they must be in the storm shelter*, she suddenly thought, but when she reached the outside refuge, she pulled and pulled at the door of the shelter but could not open it. There was no place to go but back inside the house. When Dorothy reached her room, she puzzled about what she should do next. But before she could scramble for cover, the window was blown out of the wall and came crashing down on her head. Poor Dorothy fell on the bed unconscious.

She must have been dreaming because Dorothy thought she saw some unusual things. In her mind's eye, Dorothy saw the old farmhouse effortlessly lifted from its foundation by the wind, and it was spinning wildly through the air. She looked out the window and gazed below and was terrified to see that she and Toto were in the eye of the twister. In a frightened panic, she jerked away from the window and sat on her bed. As she sat there, she hesitantly turned her eyes toward the window again, and that is when she saw things floating by that shouldn't be floating at all—cows, chickens, and that mean old Miss Gulch, riding her bicycle, laughing, and pointing her bony finger at her. Dorothy was quite unnerved by all of this and just didn't know what to make of it. She thought she must be dreaming, but it felt real.

After swirling out of control for what seemed like a terribly long time, the house landed with a jolt. Dorothy was certainly glad they had stopped spinning but was afraid of what might happen next. She worked up her courage and timidly stepped outside. Upon very close inspection of her surroundings, Dorothy confided nervously to Toto, "We're not in Kansas anymore."

A soft summer's breeze blew lazily through the trees. The sky was a beautiful azure blue, and while there was no rain predicted, there were a few small clouds innocently gathering in the east. The birds were singing, flowers were blooming, sprinklers were sprinkling, and voices of small children could be heard in the distance. "There is no school today— it's summertime!" How I loved June, July, and August when I was a child; I could sleep late, stay up late, and throw my shoes away! I only needed two things; my pink swimsuit and my favorite beach towel with *Myrtle Beach* proudly emblazoned across the center.

Oh, those wonderful, lazy, crazy days of summer. It is like welcoming a friend that has been away too long; we must spend time together and catch up on old times!

"How have you been? I'm so glad you are back! What exciting thing has happened to you since we last talked?" We ask as we sip our ice-cold glasses of homemade lemonade on the back porch swing. We listen to each other's news and eagerly wait for our turn to recount the events of the past year; there is so much to tell! A new house, a job promotion, a new baby in the family, or the future wedding of a son or daughter tops the list. After catching up on the current events of our lives, we love to reminisce years gone by. Our friendship has endured the test of time, and our hearts are warmed by each other's presence.

On days like these, we feel like we could sit for hours laughing at each other, sharing "remember when" times. "Do you remember how we used to show up at school wearing the same outfit without planning it and how we complimented each other on our 'groovy threads'?" And, "Do you remember how in ninth grade we both liked David and how he didn't even know we were alive? I can't believe he liked snooty Claire instead!" We howl, noting the last time we saw handsome David, he was completely bald but had hair growing out of his ears and nose, had a Santa Claus stomach, and was a tired, boring accountant.

As we laugh at and with each other, as old friends often do on summer afternoons, we've failed to notice the sun is no longer shining brightly; in its place is a once innocent-looking group of small clouds that has silently gathered into one huge cloud. "A bad cloud is coming up," my dad used to seriously warn. "Get in the house!" We barely made it inside before the bottom fell out. Such is the weather of summer; distant clouds that can, without warning, quietly come together and secretly brew into the worst storm of the season.

So are the storms of life.

We've all been caught in these kinds of storms. We run out on an errand and never think we might need to take our umbrella. The bright sunlight makes us squint our eyes, and the hot sun beats on our backs as we seek the refuge of our air-conditioned cars. *We sure need a shower to cool things off,* we think to ourselves and continue our errands, giving it little or no more thought. It's summer and it's supposed to be hot. But if we would only look in the distance, we would see a group of small, innocent-looking clouds floating peacefully. They may prove harmless, but they may be a storm brewing. There seems to be a lot of movement among those innocent-looking clouds, but in our haste, they are of little concern. Oblivious, we continue with our errands.

We run into the grocery store for a loaf of bread or a gallon of milk, and the minute we reach the register to pay for our purchase, we hear the rumbling and roaring of thunder and suddenly the deafening downpour of rain that no one expected. Summers are like that; rain can come at the drop of a hat and last a few short minutes. Other times, a summer shower can set in for the afternoon. I've even seen a rain shower pour out of a sunny sky. Whatever the case, we find ourselves standing on the inside looking out at the rain. Then the sad realization comes; our umbrella is in the car. We can wait it out or make a run for it. Who knows how long a summer rain will last? It may abruptly come to an end or set in for hours or even days.

In the summer of 2003, a horrifying storm blew into my life, and much like Dorothy, I failed to foresee the destruction to come. It wasn't a storm brought about by unstable weather conditions, but strong winds did blow, and the skies grew dark. Torrential rain came, and I could hear the howling wind outside my window, and the house began to shake. The rain beat relentlessly, and I was certain the glass in the windows would be blown out. *Maybe I should hide somewhere,* I thought, but where could I hide? The only safe place I could think of to hide was exactly where I was—inside my home which was built on a strong foundation and had weathered almost forty years of past storms. Others had lived in this house before us, and I knew of no tragedies in years past. But as this storm grew stronger, I could hear the house moaning and groaning under the pressure of what felt like hurricane-force winds.

Instead of blowing itself out, the storm escalated into a tornado that shook my home from its foundation, and an angry hand ripped off the roof and flung it to the ground like it was a child's toy. The hand then reached through the hole where the roof had been and pulled me into the eye of the storm. The huge funnel swirled me around, over and over, tossed me into the air, banged me against imaginary objects, and buffeted my soul. An unnerving thought crossed my mind, *This storm is going to kill me.* Round and round I went, reaching, grasping, struggling to find something to grab onto, but nothing would come within my reach. The never-ending storm continued to swirl, and I felt like a small doll being tossed higher and higher in the air. If and when I landed, where would I find myself? Two or three counties away or in a neighboring state?

Suddenly, I thought of Dorothy in *The Wizard of Oz*. This must be how she felt when she was sucked into the Kansas tornado. Her storm came up suddenly as she talked with Professor Marvel. By the time she reached home, everyone else had gone to the storm shelter, and try as she might, she would never reach safety with Auntie Em.

Poor Dorothy not only left Kansas, she went to a world she never knew existed; maybe it was somewhere over the rainbow. This was a strange world with flying monkeys, witches, and a Grand Wizard; a Cowardly Lion who desperately needed courage; a Tin Man longing for a heart; and a Scarecrow without a brain. What would happen to *me?* Like Dorothy, would I be swept away to an unknown world? Would I spend the rest of my life following that never-ending yellow brick road with its twists and turns and the song playing over and over in my head, *Follow the yellow brick road, follow the yellow brick road, follow, follow, follow, follow, follow the yellow brick road?*

Or would I be like the baby I heard about that was picked up by a tornado and then gently set down a mile away, still resting peacefully on his bed? Or would I end up like some of the people who live on the coast where hurricanes uproot huge buildings from the ground and fling them to unknown destinations? After the hurricane is over, trees are covered with shirts and pants and entire homes disappear, except for one lonely piece of furniture, like a chair or a bed. Everything else is gone without a trace.

As I twirled round and round in the tornado, a comforting thought crossed my mind and I softly whispered to myself, "If I ever get my feet on solid ground again, I'll just do what Dorothy did. I'll click the heels of my ruby red slippers together three times and confidently say, 'There's no place like home, there's no place like home'." Over and over I rehearsed the words I would say once the storm was over and my feet were on the ground. Somehow the thought comforted me. I would land and I would be safe and return to a normal life.

I briefly emerged from the imaginary storm long enough to realize two disturbing facts: I had no ruby red slippers I could tap together three times that would magically make everything like it was before, and sadly, I was already at home. Home—the place of the heart, the place where the minute you enter the door you feel the cares and problems of the day being lifted away. The weight of the world magically fades and once again you feel safe and secure. Home is the place where we are accepted and loved unconditionally, the place where we are forgiven even when we don't deserve it. It is our refuge and place of rest.

But my home and everyone in it was grieving. The walls seemed to inhale and exhale while weeping uncontrollably. The plant died and the cat hid behind the couch. It felt like a funeral home, complete with mourners. My home was torn apart, like one of those pictures you sometimes see depicting a divorced couple; a smiling couple standing embraced with one half of the picture ripped off, like you can just tear off the offending member, toss it in the trash, and go on living.

Our home had not been scarred by divorce; we were mourning the loss of our son's innocence. While at a pastorate in a small Georgia town, our seven-year-old son,

Benjamin*, had been sexually abused by a church member, and as a teenager, recently declared his sexual preference.

"I'm gay, and there is nothing you can do about it; I was born this way, and you just need to accept it," he confidently announced.

Our lives were forever changed. There would be agonizing days ahead and many sleepless nights. If only we were in *Oz*, Glinda the Good Witch might do something magical and wonderful to make it all go away. Maybe if we could make it to the Emerald City, the Wizard would turn back the hands of time and prevent our son from being molested. But we are not in *Oz* or any other make-believe place. We are in a world where good and evil war against each other. I'm not referring to fictional characters like Glinda the Good Witch of the North and the Wicked Witch of the West. I'm talking about truly evil people such as murderers, child molesters, and those who exploit others for selfish gain or pleasure. Many times innocent people, including children, are the victims of someone else's sin and the perpetual curse continues.

Three years have passed since that sad day we found out about Benjamin's abuse and his desire to live a homosexual lifestyle, and we continue to struggle along the not-so-yellow brick road that is hard and rocky. At times I feel like running away, and other times I want to throw myself over a cliff. Sometimes when I am driving, I imagine slowly but deliberately crossing the centerline and ending it all. Then I wouldn't have to hurt so much. But what good would that do? With my luck, I wouldn't die, but would only maim myself and make life harder for my family and myself. Besides, it is the coward's way out. I choose to stay and fight for my son, even though many times my strength fails and I feel like giving up. But God is rich in mercy and loving and strong. When the load is heavy and I can barely lift my head, He lifts it for me and carries me like a helpless newborn baby in the arms of her mother. He holds me close and tells me He will never leave me. He tells me he has a plan for my life and for the life of my son.

> "For I know the plans I have for you," declares the Lord, "plans to prosper you and not to harm you, plans to give you hope and a future. Then you will call upon me and come and pray to me, and I will listen to you. You will seek me and find me when you seek me with all your heart." Jeremiah 29:11–13 (NIV)

According to Romans 4:18–21, describing Abraham's certain future, even though it seemed impossible it reads,

> Against all hope, Abraham in hope believed and so became the father of many nations, just as it had been said to him, "So shall your offspring be." Without weakening in his faith, he faced the fact that his body was as good as dead—since he was about a hundred years old—and that Sarah's womb was also dead. Yet he did not waver through unbelief regarding the promise of God, but was strengthened in his faith and gave glory to God, being fully persuaded that God had power to do what he had promised. Romans 4:18–21 (NIV)

Nothing can change these promises.

I don't know what the future holds, but I know the One who holds my future and the future of my son. At the beginning of my storm, I somehow forgot this important truth. My faith wavered and I wanted to die. But living these past three years, I've come to realize God can do anything He wants to. He spoke the world into existence, He created man from a handful of dust, and He knew my name from the beginning of time. He loves me, watches over me, and blesses me abundantly, even when I don't deserve it. The fear of the unknown may trouble me, but I know I can trust the God who sent His Son to die for me and my son. For now, it is enough.

Strangers in a Strange Land

In my early parenting years, I felt like I had to be in control of every situation. I was often demanding, and I had to know where my children were at all times. I was careful about strangers and cautioned my kids not to speak to or go with anyone they didn't know. They read only wholesome literature and were not allowed to watch violent programs or movies. They were taken to church on a regular basis and were told very early that Jesus loved them and watched over them.

When my children started school, we had a five-minute devotion each morning, because I felt they needed to hear encouraging words that would help them make right decisions while they were away. We prayed before meals and said our prayers at bedtime. Our kids were not allowed to go to a friend's house if we didn't know the parents. And by that I mean really know them. Seeing them in the pick-up line at school didn't mean we knew them just because we recognized them. We wanted to know if the child's parents attended church and what their personal convictions were on such issues as alcohol, drugs, sex, and other moral issues. Basically, our children were on a short leash, and I liked it that way. All was well with my soul; I was in control. Or so I thought. After being contacted by a pastor search committee, we made a decision that would change our lives and the lives of our children forever.

It was the summer of 1994, and the temperature was

103 degrees in the shade. My husband, Mike, had accepted a pastorate in Lyola*, a small South Georgia town, and we were moving again. I had never lived below the gnat line, as it is called, and we didn't have tree frogs with sticky feet where I came from that latched onto everything, including people. Snakes were common and the folks there weren't really afraid of them but looked on them more as a nuisance. I had never seen an armadillo until we moved to the Deep South. The little town of Lyola was years behind the civilized world; dirt roads were common, and while we were there, a major conflict arose when a town official thought it was about time the citizens of Lyola, Georgia, integrated the high school prom. A front-page article in the weekly newspaper promptly squelched the notion, and the proms remained segregated.

Lyola would prove to be a strange place. One day in the future I would come to hate Lyola and wish I had never heard of such a place. But we did hear of it, and we went to live there.

When we arrived at the parsonage, a doublewide mobile home, we were met with smiling faces and willing workers to help us unload. The locals were friendly, and they later prepared an interesting meal of fish and grits when we finished unloading all of our worldly goods. I had never heard of grits with fish, but it was standard fare in the Deep South. It was even served in school lunches, and our children were unsure what to make of it all. Things were curious and strange, but we rose to the challenge and had the place looking like home in no time.

A large family in the church quickly took us in since we were strangers in a strange land and we became great friends. Being a small church, there were only two or three families with children, so our kids were glad to make instant friends with this large family, the Browns*. Our girls, Rebekah and Anna, were nine and eleven, and Benjamin was seven. The Browns had six children of various ages, and two of their girls were the same age as our girls. They spent many happy days together that summer swimming and exploring. Unfortunately, among all of their children, the Browns did not have a son Benjamin's age, but they did have a son named Derek* who was fourteen, and he took an interest in Benjamin. All of the kids said it was fine for him to tag along with the girls when they went to visit the Browns; they said they would watch over him. A stay-at-home mom, Mrs. Brown assured me Benjamin would be fine, so I felt comfortable letting him go along.

After being in Lyola several months, Benjamin went to my husband, Mike, and told him that Derek, the young boy in the Brown family who was fourteen, had touched him in a way that made him uncomfortable. Our son had been taught to tell us if anyone ever touched him in a personal area. Early on, we warned our children of the dangers of talking to a stranger, accepting anything from a stranger, and getting in the car with a stranger. While we were pleased that Benjamin had told us of the inappropriate touch, we were disturbed by it. Derek wasn't a stranger, and he and his entire family were active in the church, and they were some of our most faithful members who helped us do anything we asked. Could it have been an accident?

Mike sat down with Benjamin and quizzed him more on the subject. Had it happened before? Where were they at the time and what were they doing? Benjamin convinced Mike that it had happened only once while they were just scuffling around and maybe it was an accident. If anything remotely similar ever happened again, Benjamin was to go to his dad immediately.

We watched Derek very closely after the incident. We limited Benjamin's time with him to church time only, except for occasional visits to our home with his sisters, and we paid close attention to his whereabouts and what he was doing. Nothing out of the ordinary happened, and it looked like it was just one of those weird things that happened accidentally. Benjamin never said another word about it.

Our stay in Lyola ended after fourteen months, and I must say, I was glad to be leaving. We returned to Monroe, Georgia, the town I grew up in, August of 1995. My sister's fifteen-year-old daughter, Joy, had been diagnosed with cancer, and we felt we needed to be closer to home. A month after we arrived, my stepmother, Annie, was diagnosed with a cancerous brain tumor. Our world seemed to be crashing in around us.

Benjamin entered third grade the year we returned to Monroe. He seemed different somehow. I thought the move and all of the uncertainty in our family was making him nervous. He was extremely forgetful; almost every day he forgot to bring things home from school he needed to have—his coat, his spelling book, or a worksheet he needed to complete for homework. He often seemed to be in deep thought and stayed in his room a lot playing video games, which was the latest craze. He had to be called several times before responding; he just didn't hear his name being called. I was concerned about him spending so much time alone, but other moms with boys Benjamin's age assured me their boys did the same thing. Maybe I was overreacting due to the stress we had in our lives with the move and the diagnosis of cancer in two of our family members' lives.

I decided to watch Benjamin to see if I should be more concerned than I was. Something was bothering him, but what? Maybe he was just being a boy doing what boys do. Having only one sister, I was not as familiar with the world of boys compared with the world of girls.

During the crises our family was experiencing with the illnesses, we tried to make life as normal as we knew how. We wanted our children to feel secure amid the turmoil. My husband and I decided years before we had children that I would be a stay-at-home mom. So I did the things most stay-at-home moms do. I went to all of the parent-teacher conferences, was active in PTA, baked cookies when asked, knew my children's teachers by name and recognized them on sight. I helped with math problems, called out spelling words, and helped to create science projects, like building a volcano, and we even made a dough replica of the United States. I was a loving, involved parent. I knew my kids inside and out—their likes, dislikes, fears, and joys. I knew their strengths and weaknesses, their talents and trials. So you can imagine my concern when around age nine, my son, Benjamin, began behaving strangely. He had little or no interest in "guy" activities like basketball, baseball, football, or fishing. He was plagued with a poor self-image and was very introverted. He wore glasses, had braces, and was tall and skinny. He hated being around boys his age and was extremely intimidated by his male peers. Once he told me he didn't like being around boys because they used bad language and said mean and degrading things about girls.

I reassured myself that this was just a phase Benjamin was going through—a part of growing up. But instead of getting better, the unrest escalated. It was around fifth grade when my son confided in Mike that someone at school told him he looked gay. How can a ten-year-old kid look gay? He was very upset by the comment, and the anger within him continued to grow as his self-esteem plummeted. We assured him he was not gay and explained to him that he was a healthy, growing boy, and he would soon have his braces off and get contact lens when he was a little older. Everything would be fine, we told him. But everything wasn't fine.

Benjamin continued to be irritable, moody, and increasingly depressed. Years later we would find out that he had confided in a girl friend that he thought he was gay; everybody said he was, so it must be true. Mustn't it? What was meant to be confidential between friends became common knowledge when the friend told their classmates what Benjamin had told her and soon the label became a part of his identity. If only we had known what our son was living with, maybe we could have helped him. We remained in the dark about what was going on at school but knew something terrible was bothering Benjamin and prayed daily for wisdom to know how to help him.

Seeing our son struggling to fit in and having little confidence in himself, Mike and I tried to encourage him by pointing out his wonderful qualities; he is kind and very intelligent, he is gifted in art and very creative. He was encouraged for a while, but quickly returned to the angry mindset.

So much was going on in our lives at that time. It had been a depressing year; my niece Joy lost her battle with cancer and my stepmother's health was rapidly declining. My heart was broken over our loss, and Benjamin was constantly on my mind.

In February of 1997, we moved our church membership to a much larger church than what we had been accustomed to. There was a sizable population of boys Benjamin's age, and Mike and I desperately hoped he would make new friends. He did form a friendship with two boys at church who had loving, caring parents, and we thought he being in a new place might make the stigma of the past go away, and he would forget the feelings he had been dealing with the year before. In August the same year, Annie's battle with cancer ended. We had lost two people we loved dearly in the space of seventeen months. Things had to improve.

For a while, it looked as if things were turning around. Benjamin and his friends hung out a lot together, playing video games and having sleepovers. He seemed happier than I had seen him in some time. Mike accepted a full-time staff position at the church we attended and things were looking good. A sigh of relief was breathed, and we put the past behind us.

The middle school years followed. Everyone who has had a child in middle school knows these are turbulent times; physical and emotional changes send kids reeling, hormones rage out of control. Their feet are too big for their bodies, and their oversized hands dangle at the end of too-long arms. They are trying to figure out who they are and are extremely conscious of their appearance. Peer pressure is fierce, and the most important thing to these twelve and thirteen-year olds is being accepted and popular during the middle school years. No longer a child in elementary school, they want to feel grown up but don't know how, so they begin to behave strangely.

Suddenly, our eleven-year-old son no longer wanted to hold my hand in public, hug me or be hugged, and definitely didn't want to be kissed in front of his friends. Benjamin became secretive and asked me not to go into his room. He said he hated his school and wanted to go to a Christian school. He asked us to move the computer from his room to another location. We had placed it there because there was limited space elsewhere, and we had filtered Internet supplied by a Christian provider, and I couldn't imagine why he would ask us to move it. There was no way for him to pull up questionable sights that we didn't approve of. Mike and I had a lengthy discussion about the request. We didn't move the computer at that time, but did so a short time later. Could someone be e-mailing Benjamin things he shouldn't be viewing even with filtered Internet? What had become of the child we knew? Why did he suddenly want to change schools? Why wouldn't he do his homework?

As parents, we stood speechless and confused by the sudden changes of our preteen and were driven to distraction by something we didn't understand. The questions about homosexuality continued. Our son began saying he felt gay. As parents, we felt extreme sorrow and devastation at the very thought. Mike questioned Benjamin about his feelings, but he didn't know why he felt the way he did, he just felt gay. Mike explained to him that sometimes children may have feelings for the same sex, but it wasn't normal to be attracted to the same sex in a physical way. He showed him scripture in the Bible that condemns homosexuality and encouraged him not to think of himself that way. For a while, the talk seemed to help, but we knew Benjamin was struggling with his feelings. We were ill-equipped to deal with the problem and had nowhere to turn except to God. We continued to lift him up in prayer as we desperately searched for answers. We knew the problem wasn't over but hoped the questions and comments would just go away. Maybe if we didn't think about it, it wouldn't become true.

It would be four more years before the whole, ugly truth came out about the sexual abuse our son had endured for over a year while we were in Lyola. His peers continued to pick on him, although at the time we didn't know it. I knew something was wrong but couldn't get Benjamin to talk to me about it. There were many, many times I questioned him about his feelings, but he continued to tell me that nothing was wrong. I guess deep down I knew what was wrong, but I didn't want to believe it. I didn't want my son to be gay; I had to stop it somehow. Mike and I watched anxiously to see if Benjamin was to shake the troubling thoughts of his past. The encouraging behavior was short-lived and the anger returned with a vengeance.

Still in middle school, our son continued to behave strangely and tried to get out of gym class. He just didn't feel comfortable undressing. So he refused to dress out for gym class because he said people laughed at him. He didn't want the other boys to look at him. Every day he failed to dress out, he received a zero for gym. How can a person get a zero in gym? The only thing that is required is to put on a pair of shorts and run around, but Benjamin couldn't bear the thought of doing it.

I decided to speak to our son's favorite teacher and ask what, if anything, could be done to help Benjamin. She was kind and wonderful, just as he had said, and took it upon herself to see to it that he came to her room every day before gym class and secretly changed into shorts while she stood guard outside the door. Finally, a solution to the current madness, but shortly, another dilemma would take its place.

Benjamin began lying about his homework. He would say he had already completed it or there was no homework on that day. It wasn't long before we found out he had not done the work at all. He had no excuse. He just didn't feel like doing it. Why would a child who excelled in all subjects be content with bad grades? We had no concrete answer. Things became increasingly difficult. Benjamin said he hated himself and was angry most of the time. I begged him in tears to tell me what I could do to help him, but he would not. I now realize there was no way for him to know what he needed and neither did I.

Once Benjamin had a project to do that was relatively simple. He was to think of a favorite dish, write out the recipe, make the dish, and take it to school to share with the class. I couldn't understand a teacher giving an assignment of this kind to middle school boys—girls maybe, but boys? Benjamin didn't want to do it, big surprise there. I told him we could do it together, and we would have fun doing it. Together we picked a chocolate oatmeal cookie, one of our family's favorites and worked on it together. Once we completed the assignment, he appeared to be relieved. When I picked him up from school and asked how everything went with the cookie project, he said it went fine. Quizzing him about the container we put the cookies in, he said he forgot it. Later in the week, I found out from Benjamin's teacher that he never presented his project. He told her he didn't do it and received a zero.

"What happened to your cookies?" I asked him. Embarrassed, he said he couldn't bear the thought of standing in front of the class and talking; he threw the container and cookies in the trashcan. He threw away *chocolate*! Something really bad was going on. I was disturbed greatly and simply didn't know what to say, so I said nothing. Things snowballed from there.

The school counselor phoned one day and asked if I could come in for a meeting, which I did. The counselor revealed to me that one of Benjamin's teachers was very concerned about him. In the past, most, if not all of his teachers thought highly of him; normally he was a model student who followed directions and was pleasant to be around. Arriving at the counselor's office, I could tell she was uneasy and worried. She explained that in class one day, Benjamin started banging his head on his desk for no apparent reason. Was everything all right at home?

Suddenly, I had an out-of-body experience. I could see the counselor's lips moving and was sure she was saying something profound, but I couldn't hear her. I could see myself sitting in the chair, trying to make sense of the comments I had just heard. She continued to talk, and all I could do was weep softly. I felt like I was in Charlie Brown's classroom, listening to the teacher, "Wah, wah, wah, wah, wah." By some miracle, I pulled myself together and assured the counselor I would talk with Benjamin and try to find out what was troubling him, which I had done many times before with no success. I could barely wait to get home and see my son; I had an uncontrollable desire to grab him, gently hold him in my arms, and tell him everything would be all right even though deep down in my soul I knew there was something terribly wrong with Benjamin.

I needed help returning to my car, and it was painfully obvious that I might need a keeper if things like this continued. You know, someone to lead me around from place to place and tell me when to eat, bathe, and do other important activities. One thought circled tirelessly around my brain.

What is wrong with my child?

Crazy thoughts raced through my mind; *What is wrong with me? I thought I was a good mother, but God knows I'm not. I'm a failure as a parent. What did I do wrong?*

Irrational thoughts consumed my tired brain as I tried to think what it was I had done wrong. I convinced myself there would be a scandal. I started talking to myself. "Soon everyone will know the ugly truth. I'm not the perfect parent everyone thinks I am. People tend to think preachers' wives and families are perfect and have no problems of their own. They will never believe my perfect little family has big problems. In their eyes, I am a model mom who has it all together—like June on *Leave it to Beaver*. But I'm not as good as June Cleaver. She always kept Wally and the Beaver on the straight and narrow and looked beautiful doing it.

"I am a weak, pitiful excuse of a mother, crying my eyes out over my inadequate parenting skills. I don't and never have done dishes at seven in the morning wearing pearls and high heels like June did. I don't do housework in a sleek, designer dress like June," I wailed. I have a hard time getting dressed before noon. What would become of us? Thinking of an episode of *Beaver*, June and Ward were devastated to find out the Beav and Lumpy had skipped school to go to the circus. If that was Beaver's worst offence, I was in way over my head. How I wished that were my greatest worry.

When picking Benjamin up from school on another day, I foolishly asked him how his day was.

"Something weird happened. The sheriff and the principal came to my classroom and pulled me out into the hall. They asked me to push up my sleeves so they could see my arms. Then they asked me why I wear long sleeves all the time, and I said I like them. Can I get a snack before we go home?" I could not believe what I had just heard. What could this mean? The conversation rolled around in my brain for a few minutes, and the longer I thought about it, the madder I got. By the time we reached home, I was absolutely livid.

Trying to keep my composure, I called the school and asked to speak to the principal. He informed me that a girl Benjamin was friends with had been cutting herself, a destructive habit often associated with some form of abuse. A teacher noticed the cut marks and told the principal who in turn asked the girl why she was cutting her arms. She said that Benjamin had taught her how to do it and to go ask him, which prompted the visit to Benjamin's class. Thankfully, there was no evidence that he practiced such a destructive and disturbing behavior. I was greatly angered that someone would think they had the right to go to my son and demand he roll up his sleeves without me or my husband being present, and I informed the principal that in the future, if they had questions about my child or his actions, they had better contact me before making such accusations.

I could not believe the events that were taking place; it was like a bad dream, and I couldn't wake up. Maybe I, like Dorothy in *The Wizard of Oz*, was only dreaming, but it seemed so real. Maybe I too had been transported to another world; a parallel universe or, perhaps I had entered *The Twilight Zone*. Everything is strange there; its one bizarre event after another. In the *Zone*, people walk around

him talking, it was the alien. He had the "porch light is on, but nobody is home" look, "the wheel is spinning, but the hamster is dead" syndrome, his choo-choo jumped the tracks, and he had splinters in the windmills of his mind. I didn't know this person in my son's body. An alien evidently replaced the teacher as well. Why else would someone ask a classroom full of students to "show your work, but don't do the work." Besides, my dad was dying with cancer, and I was under unbelievable stress, and as I said these things to the principal, I began to sob uncontrollably. The poor man offered an apology for the mess my life was in, as if it were his fault.

The doom and gloom continued, and my dad died eight months later, two days after Thanksgiving. During that time, I didn't know if I would survive. The sadness over my dad was unbearable. Throughout my life I had a special relationship with my dad. I loved following him around and watching as he did things around the house, like painting and building things. I once helped him put down a hardwood floor in our living room and loved to go to the garden with him to gather the vegetables we had planted. I would miss him terribly.

Along with the roller coaster years of middle school and Benjamin's battle with homosexual desires, the trials almost did Mike and me in. Only with the Lord's help were we able to continue living. We prayed daily for Benjamin and trusted God to intervene in whatever way He chose to bring peace to his troubled soul.

As a five-year-old, our son had asked Jesus into his heart. I will never forget the day he accepted Jesus as his Savior. Since Benjamin was not in school yet because of his birthday being late in the year, he and I had taken the girls to school that morning and spent the day together just like any other day. After getting in trouble for some childish infraction, he announced that he needed Jesus in his heart. I was unsure if he indeed understood the importance of his decision, but after questioning him, I felt confident he knew what he was talking about as he gave all the right answers. When the time came for us to go pick up the girls from school, he looked out the car window toward the sky and said, "The sky looks very 'beaufitul' (his word for beautiful) today, Mom. It looks brand new." I knew God had worked a miracle in my little boy's heart.

But on several occasions while in middle school, Benjamin felt unsure of his relationship with the Lord and insisted he be baptized again. When that didn't take away the feelings of homosexuality, he talked with his youth pastor many times about his doubts and sought counsel and assurance. While we were encouraged by his concern over his salvation, there was a sense of foreboding lingering in our home. Mike and I knew the gay issue was not over.

At the end of the eighth grade, things seemed to settle down with Benjamin. Magically, one morning we awoke to find him "clothed and in his right mind." Almost overnight the unrest seemed to have vanished and his confidence returned. People do say that the middle school years are harrowing, to say the least, and I rejoiced in the fact that they were over. Benjamin was easy-going and laughed easily. He had a lot of friends—mostly girls. He was more content with his image after he had the braces removed and the glasses replaced with contact lens. He was on his way to high school, and to our relief, our son seemed at peace with himself; something we had not seen in a very long time.

Ninth grade was a breeze. Apparently, something had

changed, and all was right with the world. Benjamin made excellent grades and had a lot of friends, male and female. Was the gay issue over? He certainly felt comfortable with his peers. He was more open to hugs and kisses from us, for which we were thrilled. Relieved by and happy with Benjamin's confidence in himself, we were looking forward to the future.

Then out of nowhere, in his sophomore year of high school, things changed. Benjamin became more outspoken and open about his feelings on homosexuality. He had a determined attitude, and had made up his mind he would tell the world that he was gay. He said he had struggled a very long time with homosexual feelings and tried to make them go away, but they never would, so he had come to accept the fact that he was gay. His friends at school accepted him the way he was and we should do the same. Oh, how I wished I were Dorothy and could tap my ruby red slippers together three times and say, "There's no place like home, there's no place like home." Then I would magically be returned to the home I dearly loved.

It was a home filled with laughter and love. As I thought back over the years when our children were small, a smile came to my face. Oh, how precious our babies were! Their first teeth, first words, and their first steps flooded my mind; the first tricycle, bicycle, and roller skates, which were followed by first skinned knees. If only I could go back in time and keep our son small, I would not be living this nightmare. But one can never go back. The past is gone and the future looms ahead. Only God knows what lies before us.

The Ugly Truth Is Revealed

....

After much prayer, Mike and I went to our senior pastor and told him the story from the beginning to the end. On his advice, we sought counseling for Benjamin. We knew there was something buried deep inside him—something he would not share with us—and hoped a counselor might be able to bring it out and help him sort out the origin of his feelings. We talked to our son about going to counseling, and surprisingly he agreed to go. With the appointment made, Mike and Benjamin traveled the twenty miles to the counselor's office, and the truth finally came out. I waited at home, thinking the counselor was a miracle worker and he would be able to fix our son.

After what seemed like eternity, the pair returned. I knew the minute my husband walked in the door something horrible had happened. Benjamin went upstairs to his room, and Mike called me into the den with a look on his face I will never forget. It was a sad face filled with fear and pain. Nothing could have prepared me for what I would hear. I waited for my husband to speak, but he just couldn't say the words. Finally, he managed to say, "Benjamin was sexually abused by Derek while we were in Lyola." In shocking disbelief, I tried to process the information I had just received, but I couldn't bear to think that such a thing had happened to our son. I felt sick to my stomach as waves of nausea swept over me, and momentarily I felt like I might faint. I was knocked to my knees, and I felt like a giant ocean wave was pulling me under, deeper and deeper. How can such a thing happen to a pastor's son by a church member? Where was I when it happened? Where did the abuse take place? Where was my son's guardian angel everyone says children have? And the hardest, most painful question of all, where was God? In anger I cried out to God, "God why? Where were you, and why did you let this happen? He was only seven years old, just a little boy. You are supposed to protect the little ones. You said, 'And whosoever shall offend one of these little ones that believe in me, it is better for him that a millstone were hanged about his neck, and he were cast into the sea'" (Mark 9:42 KJV). Why, God, do you let people sexually abuse small children who can't defend themselves? Why do the defenseless ones have no one to defend them? How could you let this happen; where are you, God, where are you?"

In confusion and disbelief, I cried, "Lord, as the wife of a minister, I have been required to make sacrifices; days or nights are spent alone while my husband attends to the sick or the dying. Some evenings I sit alone while he counsels a couple with marital or financial problems. I've moved to places where I didn't know a soul; I've lived in places less than adequate, and left my family hundreds of miles away and lived on meager incomes. I've painted walls, cut acres of grass around the church, fed and entertained missionaries, and encouraged fellow servants. I'm not complaining, Lord, I did these things because I love you and want to serve you. My heart's desire is to be a faithful daughter to you and a supportive wife for my husband." I felt wounded and very alone. Then in a still, small voice God said to me, "Do you think you deserve special treatment because you are the wife of a minister? Should you be exempt from problems and hardships because you are my servant? How do you expect to feel the pain of others if you never feel pain yourself?"

Ashamed of my angry outburst, I asked the Lord to help me understand. I suddenly thought of Job and his great losses and many trials. The apostle Paul spent many nights in prison and suffered with physical problems, yet he states in 2 Corinthians his dependence on God.

> We do not want you to be uninformed, brothers, about the hardships we suffered in the province of Asia. We were under great pressure, far beyond our ability to endure, so that we despaired even of life. Indeed, in our hearts we felt the sentence of death. But this happened that we might not rely on ourselves but on God, who raises the dead. 2 Corinthians 1:8–9 (NIV)

What about Jesus? He was perfect and without sin, God in the flesh; one would think his life would be without pain or sadness, yet his destiny was the cross. He came to die for the sins of every man, and yes, even for the child molester.

Strangely, a verse of scripture came to my mind in I Thessalonians 5:16–18 (NIV), "Be joyful always; pray continually, give thanks in all circumstances, for this is God's will for you in Christ Jesus." Disturbed by this verse, I cried out, "Lord, how am I supposed to be thankful for something as horrible as this? Surely you didn't mean for me to be thankful for the bad things, did you, Lord?" To which he replied, "I didn't say be thankful *for* the bad things, I said to be thankful *in* all things, good and bad." Confused, I asked, "Lord, does Romans 8:28 hold true to something as heartbreaking as sexual abuse? Will this life-altering experience truly compel us to say, 'We know in all things God works for the good of those who love him?'" In anguish, my heart cried out, "How can any good come from this? No one can benefit from sexual abuse; there is nothing but devastation and pain." But deep in my heart I knew God's Word was my only hope; if I couldn't believe and trust his Word, I had no hope at all. "I don't understand, God, my heart feels like it has been ripped apart and is laid bare. I can't breathe, please help me."

After eight years, we finally knew the truth. It all made sense now; the anger, depression, and self-hatred Benjamin expressed was the result of sexual abuse. My husband and I cried for a very long time, each of us thinking it was our fault. I was an overbearing mother and knew that I was responsible for driving him into the arms of another man. Mike insisted it was his fault since he worked twelve hour days and spent little time with Benjamin. Back and forth we argued about whose fault it was. For many months the guilt would continue to haunt us, and we didn't know if we had the stamina for such a trial.

It was evident we needed to sit down with our girls and tell them what had happened, but we dreaded it greatly. They knew something was terribly wrong; they had never seen either of us so upset. How would we tell them? Where would we start? We realized we had to start at the beginning, the first inappropriate touch that escalated into continual sexual abuse. We called a family meeting and told Anna and Beka about the abuse, the gay feelings, and the counseling. They were very distraught and visibly shaken to their core. We couldn't speak. No words would come, so we sat and cried together. Slowly, one by one, we left each other and went to our bedrooms to mourn in private.

The following days were filled with more crying and wandering around the house in a depressed state, not knowing what we should do. I couldn't sleep at night because every time I closed my eyes, I saw Benjamin as a seven-year-old boy, being repeatedly victimized; the fear and guilt so apparent on his sweet, round face. His youthful innocence shattered and God's design for a healthy sexual relationship between a husband and wife was now distorted and twisted. I felt like my son had been sacrificed on the altar of sexual perversion. His sense of natural affection now warped for all time and eternity.

What would become of him? Our hopes and dreams for him now broken and destroyed. Because of the abuse and subsequent homosexuality, Benjamin might never have a wife to love, never have children of his own, and he would die a lonely, bitter old man. Grief would dominate our lives forever, and I felt like someone I dearly loved had died; only there was no closure as in death, just a continual feeling of grief and loss.

When someone you love is gay, the pain and sadness never leave. Just when you think you have come to terms with the issue, a bigger, stronger wave of grief washes over you, knocks you down, and pulls you under. As you sink deeper and deeper, you struggle to reach out and grab onto something that will save you, but nothing is there. Sometimes you are glad nothing can save you. You just want the pain to go away.

A strange thing happened while I was grieving. My heavenly Father impressed upon my heart that he too had a Son who was sacrificed. But his Son was offered for my sin and the sins of the world. He died for any and every one who will call out to him for forgiveness—for me, for you, and yes, even the child molester. As I sat thinking about Jesus' sacrifice, I wondered how the Father felt when he sent his only Son to die for people like me. How his heart must have grieved. He gave his precious Son; the perfect for the imperfect, the sinless for the sinful. He came to die for an unlovely, ungrateful, and undeserving humanity. I can understand why God had to turn his head away at the cross; it simply was too painful to watch. Every time I looked in my precious baby boy's face, I felt pain. It felt like I would never be able to erase that image from my mind. I too had to turn my face away; the pain was too great to endure.

I tried to think back over the fourteen months when we were in Lyola. Over and over in my mind I replayed things that were said and done; decisions and choices I had made as a parent, searching for answers. How could a young boy be victimized right under his parents' noses? Desperately I searched my memory for hints, warning signs, or red flags, but being unfamiliar with such signs, I just didn't see it coming. Derek was sort of a loner, but I justified that behavior due to the fact that he was the only boy among so many girls.

What seemed to be an odd time for such thoughts, memories of my childhood came to mind. I remembered living near a little country store operated by a very old lady, Mrs. Akins, who had a wonderful wooden and glass cabinet filled with all sorts of candy that cost only a few pennies. My dad took my sister and me to the store on a regular basis, and we were presented with a very tiny brown paper bag that we could fill with fireballs, small wax bottles we had to bite the tops off of to get to the grape and cherry liquid inside, wax lips, and bubble gum. It was what we lived for. Other fond memories came to my mind, such as making mud pies and pretending to eat them, catching lightning bugs and placing them in jars or wearing them as rings, collecting bugs for a bug collection, and star-gazing at night looking for the Big Dipper; my first bike without training wheels, my first puppy that was so small he fit in the palm of my dad's large hand, and the beautiful yellow galoshes I loved to wear when it was raining. Such tender and warm memories I have of my childhood; these barely scratch the surface.

What kind of memories would Benjamin have? Would the memories of his first seven years be forgotten amid the turmoil that followed? Would he only remember shame, guilt, and anger? Was our son ever threatened by his abuser or warned not to tell? Did he experience nightmares and secretly think of suicide? Would the happy times be a distant memory that he could not relate to?

I hope not, I pray not. I desperately need to know that he will remember the happy times, times that warm his heart and make him feel loved, like the time he won an art contest in first grade and had his picture in the newspaper, which I have framed and in our dining room to this day, and the Christmas when he was eight and received his Super Nintendo he longed and begged for and was so happy he cried tears of joy; his first cowboy boots, cowboy hat, and cap pistol, his much-loved rocking horse and Big Wheel, Sit and Spin, and big bike. God, please help my son know that he is loved and nothing or no one can ever change that.

The Darkest of Days

··

I soon became physically ill. I was plagued with diarrhea
and nausea. Every time I ate I grew deathly sick and lived
on Imodium. Soon the home would come and get me. I
could forget my troubles in "the home." They would give
me drugs to make me forget. Daily they would feed me,
give me my medication, and pat me on the head. If I was
good, they might let me weave a basket or pick flowers. I
eagerly awaited their arrival.

To compound the problem of my condition, our vacation week drew near. Since we had reservations and had
paid for the condominium at the beach, we had to go. The
excitement that usually accompanied our annual beach trip
was painfully absent. Halfheartedly, we packed our bags
and left.

The road trip was a disaster; still overwhelmed with
the nausea, I rode with my face positioned in front of
the air conditioning vent and breathed deeply. The cool
air eased the nausea and enabled me to continue the trip.
Occasionally, I hung my head out the window like a dog,
hoping to be knocked unconscious by the 75 mile an hour
wind that whipped past me as we sped along the interstate.
If I was unconscious or maybe plagued with a temporary
case of amnesia, I would be able to forget our current crisis. I could go on to the beach and enjoy the trip because I
wouldn't remember any of the terrible details of the recent
weeks. But instead of amnesia, reality kept slapping me

in the face, because every few miles I thought I would be sick, so we stopped at every rest area between Georgia and Florida. And to make things worse, we had promised some old friends who lived about halfway to the beach that we would stop for a visit. Since they were expecting us and had made plans for the visit, we felt like we had to go.

Arriving at their home, we feigned joy and excitement. We talked over old times and caught each other up on recent news. "By the way, did I tell you that Benjamin is gay? Yes, we just found out a few weeks ago, and oh, did I mention he was sexually abused as a child?" (No, I didn't really tell them that, even though it was foremost on my mind). It was a dreadful mistake going there; we were not good company although we tried to appear normal. We told them we were in a hurry to get going, but they insisted we grab some fast food before we left. After all, we had not seen each other in years and rarely got to visit. Stupidly, we agreed to go. As we sat at the local burger place, Benjamin decided he needed to go to the men's room and was gone longer than I thought he should be gone. Wild with fear, I sat in that seat and continued the small talk.

All I could think of was there must be a child predator lurking in one of the stalls, waiting for someone to come in alone. In my mind, I saw a small boy of seven walking toward the well-hidden abuser. I just couldn't remember that Benjamin was fifteen years old; he seemed so small. My heart began to race and my stomach tightened into a knot. I wanted to bolt for the men's room but decided that would be a bad move. So I waited. When I could wait no more, I sent my husband in after him. Shortly, they came out and returned to the table. Surely this seemed like freaky behavior to our friends, but I didn't care; I wanted to make sure Benjamin was safe. We went to a hotel for the night and planned to finish the trip in the morning.

We only had about two hours left to our destination, so everyone eagerly awoke the next morning to finish the last leg of the trip. When we arrived at the beach, everyone seemed to relax. The sun, the beach, and the ocean temporarily made our troubles melt away. I don't know why, but the sea often has a tranquil and soothing effect. Hopefully, I would be able to relax and forget my troubles for the next seven days.

Unfortunately, the sickness continued the entire week of vacation, and I hung out in the bedroom a lot while Mike and Benjamin walked along the beach talking. I prayed for a miracle, but one didn't come. I just wanted to be normal again, whatever that was. How can a person know what normal is? I mean, how do we know what to compare our lives with and who is a good example of normal? The answers to these questions persistently eluded me.

I guess if we compared ourselves with someone else, they might say that we are normal; maybe being gay is not that big of a deal. My son has never murdered anyone or robbed a bank or physically abused anyone. But can we truthfully say we are not as bad as someone else because we haven't done the things they have done? After much meditation, I realized the only person we should ever compare ourselves to is the person of Christ. We aren't supposed to excuse our sins. As Christians, our standard to live by is Jesus Christ and anything less is not good enough. He is our example; we should strive to be conformed to his likeness. Lesson taken.

Vacation week finally ended, and we returned home to find things exactly like we left them. I was still physically ill and couldn't eat. I needed to think positive thoughts; maybe I would lose some weight.

In July, shortly after our vacation, we celebrated our 27th wedding anniversary. On the Friday before our anniversary, my husband came in from work and said, "I've had it with all of our problems; I'm leaving!" He then proceeded to pull down the attic stairs, climb up and throw down the luggage. I stood in shock and timidly asked him where he was going and he said we were going on a trip. Relieved I was to accompany him, I asked, "A trip? Where?" The past few weeks had been so disturbing, I had forgotten our anniversary was that same weekend. Mike surprised me by taking me to a posh resort to celebrate. He looked so pleased with himself I couldn't bear to tell him that I didn't feel good and didn't feel like celebrating, so off we went. We tried to have a good time but both of us wondered why we were even there. Anniversaries are supposed to be happy times, but it was too difficult to forget what was going on back home. Secretly I feared that Benjamin might take the opportunity to run away while we were gone, and I wondered if we would truly be able to celebrate anything ever again.

The weekend over, we returned home to find that Benjamin had not run away but was sitting in his room doing whatever it was that he did. Now that the truth was out, new revelations occurred at an uncomfortable pace. One afternoon, Benjamin and I had some time to talk, and he stunned me by saying that he was angry with his dad for not spending enough time with him when he was younger. He said he wanted to hurt his dad because he had failed to spend time with him, which wasn't at all true. Even though Mike worked very long hours, he tried unsuccessfully to engage our son in basketball, tennis, and fishing. He played video games with him when he could and often horsed around outside in the pool.

Early in our marriage we made the decision not to put our children in day care if we could avoid it. Since I had been raised in a home where both parents worked, I was allowed too much free time to get into trouble and made some bad decisions because there was no parent at home to stop me. I wanted more for our children, and my husband made great sacrifices so I could stay at home with our children. We believed we were doing what was best for them, especially during their early years.

Where was Benjamin getting these strange ideas? Maybe he was trying to sort things out in his head, and it was the only thing he could come up with. Since he denied the sexual abuse was largely responsible for his homosexual feelings, he had to find another reason to blame it on. It didn't make sense. Was he trying to transfer the guilt and shame to Mike instead of where it belonged? Was he trying to validate his desires?

As opportunities presented themselves, Mike and I tried to engage our son in conversation. The counselor said it was good to encourage him to put his feelings into words. On one such occasion, he admitted to us that he had been angry for almost eight years. He was angry with God because he didn't protect him, and he had been angry with Derek for what he had done to him. He was especially angry with God because he prayed over and over for God to take his homosexual feelings away, but he didn't help him. He was still angry with Derek for abusing him but was working on getting over the anger. To sit and listen to your child tell you that he asked God for help, but God didn't help him, was one of the saddest and most painful things I've ever experienced. My heart broke as I cried out to God, "Why, God, didn't you help my son?" I wondered if there could be a purpose in this dreadful experience. Could God take something so despicable and sickening as sexual abuse and use it for good? I couldn't understand how something so hideous could ever be turned into something positive. I knew what Romans 8:28 said, but it made me sick to think about it.

There are no words in the English or any other language that could describe how Mike and I felt. Feelings of guilt, inadequacy, and shame tortured us; shame that we could let something so vile happen on our watch. God had entrusted three small children to us, and we had failed him. We felt like someone we loved had died, only worse. They say time heals all wounds, but if we had all of eternity to heal from this, it would only begin to scratch the surface. Surely, it is more than a mom or dad can bear.

My sad existence vacillated between anger and numbness; my heart was raw and my nerves were on the outside of my skin and were over-stimulated by every noise, emotion, and the slightest touch. Would I ever get better? I cried all the time, and some days I called my husband at the church and wept into the phone while he told me to get control of myself. Each morning as soon as I opened my eyes, the tears would come. I was a mess and couldn't do anything right. I tried to do laundry, but messed it up too. In a zombie state, I would put in the detergent, add the clothes, and walk away. Hours later, I returned to check on it only to find I had never closed the lid; the machine won't start unless the lid is closed.

I wandered aimlessly from room to room, wondering what it was I was looking for. The grocery store was one of the hardest jobs; it took days to make the list, and when I finally got there, I couldn't concentrate. *Where do they keep the milk?* After meandering around for hours, I triumphantly made it to the register. One small victory, yes, but the job wasn't completed. After loading the stuff into the cart, I now had to unload the stuff onto the belt, reload it into the cart again, unload the stuff and put it in the car, unload the car and take everything inside, and finally put it all away, assuming I remembered where everything belonged. I thought of Dorothy and the Scarecrow in *The Wizard of Oz* and hopelessly thought, *If I only had a brain.*

I sat on the sofa all day and didn't care if I got up or not. I've always been a fanatic about the house, a place for everything and everything in its place. A clean house always made me feel wonderful. Who cares now? Nobody. I went weeks without vacuuming, mopping, or dusting. The dust and I had an understanding. If it didn't bother me, I wouldn't bother it. We could dwell together in unity. Clutter piled up everywhere. I just didn't care. I had bigger fish to fry. Having a gay son will certainly help you put things in perspective. Suddenly, dishes didn't matter, dirty sheets didn't matter, and laundry didn't matter. Nothing matters anymore except my son and the mess he's in.

Along with not caring about anything, I became extremely claustrophobic. Have you ever been afraid of the shower? For a while I couldn't take a shower because it felt like everything was closing in on me. The glass shower doors had to go. They made me feel like a prisoner behind them, so I bought a clear shower curtain. As long as I could see something else besides the white walls, I was all right. I really should have been in counseling myself, and for a brief moment, I considered it, but what good would it do? I would only sit and cry.

Later that same year, (the year from you know where), a weird thing happened to my throat. I felt like I was choking when I swallowed. If I took a pill, it felt like it got stuck half way down. My family doctor referred me to an ear, nose, and throat person. He decided to check my thyroid gland and everything was normal. Next, he wanted to put me to sleep and poke around in my throat and look around, which sounded like an exciting way to spend the day. I was okay with that because I would be asleep for most of the day, and if you're asleep, you don't have to think about anything. While looking around in my throat, the doctor spied some red lesions and sent them to the lab for further scrutiny. Praise God, they were not cancer. The doctor didn't know exactly what they were, just what they weren't. They probably came from all the weeping and wailing I had been doing.

The whole family was on edge and snappy. I think it was a self-defense tactic we used to scare the other person into not saying whatever it was they wanted to say. I think we all were afraid that it might be something we didn't want to know. And if we didn't hear the bad news, we could continue to function.

Benjamin came home from school one day, and we struck up a conversation. He told me through tears that he really didn't mean what he said about his dad. He was a good dad, and he didn't know why, but he wanted to punish him somehow. It worked. He felt badly about it, and even though Mike felt better about it when I told him Benjamin was sorry, I could tell he was hurting inside. Words can do so much harm. We can apologize for things we say, but sadly, the damage has already been done. People can forgive us when we hurt them with our words, but the pain is there for a long time.

I read somewhere that words are like a big, fluffy pillow. If you tear open the pillow and let the wind take the feathers away, there is no chance on earth or heaven that you could ever collect them back again. They have been blown in many different directions; there is no way to find them all. Our words are like that. We speak them carelessly, and then they are gone on the wind. There is no way to take them back, but thankfully, there are people who are gracious enough to forgive and most importantly forget.

Have you ever heard someone say, "Well, I can forgive, but I can never forget"? To me, that is not true forgiveness. We can control our thoughts if we want to. The problem is, sometimes we want to continue nursing our hurt feelings and feeling sorry for ourselves. Why can't we be more like God? If a repentant heart turns to God and asks for forgiveness, God will forgive. And not only does he forgive, he forgets. "As far as the east is from the west, so far has he removed our transgressions from us" (Psalm 103:12 NIV).

It was evident to us that Benjamin's thoughts were confused and uncertain; we could see the wheels turning in his head. Many times he lashed out and later apologized. His troubled thoughts turned into harsh words, which he later regretted. We knew the school environment he was in and the friends he had at the public school had a strong influence on him. After much prayer and consideration, Mike and I decided to pull Benjamin out of public school and put him in a Christian school in his junior year of high school. It was probably too little, too late, but we did it anyway. The Christian school gave us the pastor's discount, but we still had to take out a second mortgage on our house. We knew we were grabbing at straws, but we pressed on hoping and praying that in some way things might change.

Before accepting Benjamin into the school, Mike and I had to go to an interview with the principal and tell her why at this late date we wanted to put him in Christian school. We began to explain about the abuse and how we hoped it might help him if he was in a Christian environment. I was a complete mess and cried throughout the interview. Meanwhile, Benjamin was taking the entrance exams and did extremely well.

The beginning of the school year drew near, and our son was getting nervous. He was afraid the kids might not be friendly. All of his friends at the public school knew he was not returning but would be attending a Christian school in the fall. People everywhere wanted to know why he was changing. People at church, friends, and family seemed confused. Why would he change schools when he already had his class ring from the public school? Who changes schools when you have only two years left? I managed to make a lame excuse and do it without squalling.

I contemplated getting a job but soon realized no one in their right mind would hire a distraught person such as myself. It was obvious I wasn't mentally capable of doing anything. I couldn't even do laundry correctly, why would I think I could perform a new task efficiently? Besides, I was easily distracted and couldn't make simple decisions like what kind of toothpaste to buy.

The first day of school arrived, and Benjamin did fine. He appeared to be feeling better about the change. After two days of school, he mysteriously felt quite ill and didn't want to go. The next day, there was a miraculous recovery, and he went to school. Along with the vacillating opinions of the new school, Benjamin also wavered in practically every other decision he made. He just didn't know what he wanted or why.

It didn't matter whether Benjamin was at home, school, or any other place; my thoughts were consumed with him. It didn't matter what I was doing, he was constantly on my mind. I was at a loss to understand how a twelve or thirteen-year-old boy could deal with the baggage he had to deal with and yet continue to function. It broke my heart to think how Benjamin carried the emotional baggage around, day after day, hurting inside, and not being able to get the help he needed. How did it make him feel to think God had abandoned him? Who could he trust, would he ever get past the pain? How he must have felt so alone in his troubled soul, it breaks my heart to think about it. In his mind, he must have felt deserted by God and us. He knew our view on homosexuality, and it was not encouraging. How did he face each day without wanting to end his life? To our shock, we would find out later from the counselor that Benjamin had indeed felt suicidal and had considered it on several occasions in middle school. Surely God had intervened and prevented him from carrying it out.

In my mind I wondered if we had pressed Benjamin more about the inappropriate touch incident, maybe he would have told us the truth. But looking back, I know we didn't want to know the truth because the truth was too ugly, and we didn't want to believe it could happen to us.

Today I marvel at God's grace and love during the troublesome middle school years. It truly is a miracle Benjamin didn't commit suicide even though he strongly considered it. My heart aches every time I think what he must have gone through, the feelings of shame, guilt, rejection, and loneliness. How I wish I could go back and relive those years armed with the information I now have. I would do things differently that time around. I would love him more and punish him less. I would kiss him and hug him every time I could and tell him I love him no matter what. I would promise him he could tell me anything, and I would do everything in my power to fix the brokenness. I would tell him that nothing he could tell me would ever lessen my love for him, and I mean nothing. I can't go back, but I can change my attitudes and actions in the here and now. Instead of criticism, I can offer him unconditional love that will never be withheld for any reason.

Things seemed to be settling down a bit. Benjamin's junior class trip was scheduled September 2–5, and he had serious doubts about going, but the trip was mandatory. He became restless and worried; the thought of going on a trip with other guys unnerved him considerably. We tried to encourage him, telling him he would have a good time and how it would be a chance to get better acquainted with the other students. Benjamin struggled and brooded over his decision until the day of the trip. When the day arrived, Benjamin seemed all right with going. We rose early and had a light breakfast. All systems go. As we loaded his luggage in the van, he became painfully quiet. Before we could back out of the driveway, he suddenly became sick and threw up in the front yard. There we stood, watching him. My insides ached for him, but we didn't know what to do. I said we would call the school and tell them he was sick. He said no, he would be fine in a little while. We went back inside and waited while he continued to be sick. Almost in tears, he said he just couldn't go on the trip. We tried to encourage him but said the final decision would be his.

Mike and I sat quietly on the sofa and waited. What could we do to help him? Finally, we heard him brushing his teeth and gargle. He emerged from the bathroom and announced that he was ready to go. All the way to the school I fought back tears and tried to smile and assure him it wouldn't be that bad and maybe he might connect with a friend. Oh, how I wished that would happen! If only he could make one friend, I felt he could adapt to his new surroundings. These and other thoughts crowded my mind as we drove to the school. No one said anything; the ride was eerily quiet. Mike was stressed, I was stressed, and Benjamin was stressed. Secretly I hoped the bus had left without him and we could take him back home, but they were there waiting. We helped him take his bag inside the gym and suddenly he said, "Bye, see you in a few days." That's it. He walked away and into the group. No hug, no anything. I wanted to grab him and tell him he didn't have to go, but I didn't. We got into the van and drove home. Unbidden, the tears began to flow freely; I felt like I had abandoned my son. My chest hurt and I worried that something would happen to my now sixteen-year-old son, who strangely looked like a small, scared seven-year-old in my mind. I prayed earnestly for God to protect him.

The first night Benjamin was away, I woke in the middle of the night with a panic attack. Horrible dreams disturbed my sleep, my chest was hurting, and I thought I was having a heart attack but knew the reason my heart hurt was because it was breaking and it wanted to die so it wouldn't feel the pain anymore.

Maybe if I could make it to the Emerald City, the

Wizard in *The Wizard of Oz* could give me a new heart; one that would be more durable and would never break again. Each day I half expected the school to call and tell us to come and pick up Benjamin, but it didn't happen. Several more days passed, and there was no word from him. Maybe that was a good sign. The day finally came for the class to return, and I could hardly wait to see my son. Mike and I got to the school early and sat staring down the highway. We parked so we could see the bus when it rounded the curve. Soon we saw the big yellow bus; we were both excited and nervous. Two things could happen. Benjamin might say he had a great time and was glad he went, or he could say he had a terrible time and really didn't like us anymore. Gratefully, it was the former. He told us everything they did and seemed quite excited about the whole thing!

The next day was Benjamin's seventeenth birthday, so we took him to his favorite restaurant where he devoured the seafood platter. Watching him sitting there, I could barely believe he was seventeen. The window of influence was growing smaller and smaller. Another year and he would be finished with high school and off to college. I didn't even want to think about that; the freedom it would allow him coupled with the distance from home unnerved me. He could do whatever he wanted, and we would be none the wiser.

Life returned to some semblance of normalcy. Benjamin seemed to be settling in at the new school and was in a good mood when I picked him up each day. Although he did experience mood swings, they seemed to be getting farther apart. After church visitation on a Monday night, Benjamin acted disturbed about something but didn't want to talk to me. He said he would talk to his dad later. When Mike got home, they went into our son's room and shut the door. They were in there a very long time, and even though I had my ear pressed to the door, I couldn't make out a thing. All I could hear were soft words being spoken. When the door opened, a distraught dad emerged. Benjamin went on to bed, and we had some time to discuss the latest bombshell.

Benjamin, having been in church since he was a few days old, had decided he didn't believe in God at all and only said he did because he knew we wanted him to.

He said the Bible was wrong about homosexuality, and every time he went to church, he felt like a hypocrite because he didn't agree with anything our pastor said. He said he thought he would visit other churches because there are some nonjudgmental ones around. Why can't we just accept him the way he is? Being gay feels right to him he said. I cried out in pain and thought to myself, *Would someone please shoot me, run over me with a tractor-trailer, or throw me off a cliff? I really don't want to live anymore; it is just too painful!* We stood looking at each other without any words to say. So we said nothing, looked into each other's sad eyes, and went to bed.

The next morning, Mike told me he had a very disturbing dream the night before. I couldn't believe what I was hearing because he very rarely remembers any dreams at all. I was afraid to ask what the dream was about, but I did anyway, and was relieved when he refused to tell it. As if it were not enough to deal with the problem during waking hours, we were also tortured in our dreams.

I felt like someone I loved very much had died.

The Miracle of the Baby Squirrel

....

A couple of days later during my quiet time, God spoke to me John 5:39 (KJV); "Search the scriptures; for in them ye think ye have eternal life: and they are they which testify of me." I got the bright idea to compile an extensive list of verses that might help Benjamin. Everything I could find on the mind and how it is such a battlefield, I typed. Every verse that spoke of our minds and how the enemy desires to invade our thought life, I also typed on this very long list. Verses on deception were added, and how we can have perfect peace by keeping "our minds on Him" (Isaiah 26:3 KJV).

I left the list on the dresser in his room, like it was a gift. To say that he was not appreciative would be putting it mildly. After Benjamin got home from school and found the "gift," he launched into a tirade about how he didn't believe the Bible anymore. An instant replay of the latest bombshell from a couple of nights earlier stabbed me to the core of my being. Weeping, I told him if he didn't believe in God, he couldn't know the Lord, and if he didn't know the Lord, he would be lost for all time and eternity—separated from God and us. He seemed unfazed by my words. I couldn't let myself think about it, it was just too sad.

Wednesday night Bible study came, and I couldn't bring myself to go. I was amazed at my husband and his ability to continue to teach his Wednesday night class and not crumble in front of the class. I knew if I went to class and someone asked me if something was wrong, I would end up in tears. Only our pastor and a few people knew what we were going through. I couldn't blurt out the truth of the abuse and homosexuality. We continued to keep up appearances, but at times felt like we were living a lie. To share our pain with our church congregation would be devastating. They wouldn't understand.

Benjamin started worrying about what I had said to him earlier about being lost forever. He wanted to talk to his dad after church and told him he didn't really mean what he had said about not believing in God; he was just upset. At least he was thinking.

After experiencing the devastation of the past several months, I was in desperate need of some time with the Lord on an extended basis. The fall retreat the ladies of our church attended each year was just around the corner. I had mixed emotions about going, but I knew I would be blessed beyond measure if I decided to go. Weeks before time to leave, I argued back and forth within myself; go, stay, go, stay. I decided to go. When the day arrived, and I really didn't feel like going, Mike urged me on; "It will be good for you." Even though I was a nervous wreck and a mess of an individual, I went. I prayed for a time of blessing and healing for myself. I was still very emotional but hoped no one would notice as we traveled along to our destination.

After we arrived at our villa, we freshened up and headed out for dinner. I ate very little and managed to engage in somewhat intelligent conversation. The evening session followed dinner, and even though the evening was inspiring, I felt like I was carrying the weight of the world on my shoulders. No one questioned the mood I was in, of which I was grateful. When the evening session was over,

we met together for a time of sharing and prayer. Several
ladies shared specific prayer requests concerning "giants" in
their lives that needed to be slain. I wanted to share my
giant but was afraid of what people might think. After all,
I was a minister's wife. Telling other women that your son
was sexually abused as a child and now thinks he is gay just
isn't the kind of prayer request most people would agree to
share.

Foremost on our minds was a sister in the Lord who
was facing surgery for thyroid cancer. We surrounded her
and prayed. In that type of atmosphere, I could weep freely
as other women wept too. It was such a relief to empty
myself of all of the emotions that were stirring within me.
There were prayers for those dealing with grief, wayward
sons and daughters, and estranged husbands. I wanted to
tell them about Benjamin and ask for the prayers of my
sisters in Christ and feel the compassion they so freely were
giving but just couldn't. I was too afraid they would find out
that I was not perfect and just because I was a pastor's wife
didn't mean my life was perfect either.

Why are we afraid to let people know "the real me,"
to put ourselves in a position of vulnerability? We all want
to be loved and respected by our peers, but sometimes we
have to come clean with God and ourselves. I felt like I was
lying to my sisters in Christ because I had a terrible secret
that I didn't want them to know. I didn't want to admit it,
but I knew I would never have complete release and healing until I purged myself of my secret. I just couldn't do it
right then.

After the conference, I returned rested and encouraged.
My husband had a big surprise waiting for me when I got
home. There is nothing I love more than a screened porch.

THERE'S NO PLACE LIKE HOME

We had talked about building one for years, but had put it off. While I was away, Mike and Benjamin started work on a screened porch for me! I couldn't believe they had accomplished so much in two days. It wasn't finished, but there was a roof on it, and I have spent many, many mornings out there, listening to the birds and momentarily forgetting all my troubles.

By this time, it was late September, and the mornings were cool and refreshing. As soon as I got up and had my cup of tea, I headed to the porch with my Bible. It would be spring before the porch was painted and screened, but it was like an oasis for me. I had my card table set up with a folding chair and felt like I was in heaven. It's amazing what a difference it makes, just being outside. I could breathe easier, think clearer, and God has revealed many spiritual truths to me on my porch.

One day I witnessed an unbelievable event. Annabelle, one of our cats, seemed to be attacking something in the back yard, so I went to investigate. A baby squirrel had fallen from its nest, and the cat was trying to eat it! The baby screamed for its mother, but she didn't dare leave the safety of the nest. I scooped up the cat and put her inside and decided to call the local veterinarian and inquire as to how I should proceed. The vet told me that the baby was probably hurt badly, falling from very high up from his nest, and the mother would probably leave him there to die. I begged her to come and get it and doctor it, but she said he wouldn't live. I went back to the porch to see what might happen next.

There he was, scared half to death. I got the idea of picking up the baby and trying to doctor it myself. I thought if I could get him, I could feed him with an eyedropper like they do at the vet when they have tiny kittens, and he might live. But as I got closer to the baby, he screamed his little head off. I was afraid to get too close, so I got the idea of spraying the baby with the garden hose to make him run toward the tree from which he had fallen. He ran a little bit but didn't realize he was so close to his home, way up in the top of the oak tree. I sprayed a little more, and finally he noticed he was at the tree. He started crying for his mommy, over and over, and somehow managed to scamper up the tree about three or four feet. I couldn't believe what my eyes witnessed next; the mother squirrel came swiftly down the tree, checked her precious baby over and gently bundled him up underneath her mama squirrel chin and ran back up the tree! I found myself cheering loudly for the mother and her baby. "Run back to the nest with your mom, you'll be safe there!"

I had witnessed a miracle of God. I sensed him saying to me, "If I can take a baby squirrel back to his nest, high up in a tree unharmed, I can bring your baby back to your nest the same." I stood there in awe of what I had just seen happen. I was laughing and crying at the same time and praising God for the glimpse of what lies ahead for my baby. God can take away the guilt, doubt, confusion, and anger from my baby and restore his confidence, peace, and joy. God can bring healing where there is pain and replace the hate with his love. I couldn't help but tell God, "Thank you for saving the baby squirrel and thank you for saving my baby, because one day I know everything will be all right. Benjamin will be recovered, rescued, safe, and secure. I know you love me and my baby because you made this happen just for me."

With new courage, I decided I could make it to choir

practice that evening. After practice was over, a friend asked me to stay behind for a few minutes because she wanted to talk to me about something. Close to tears, she said, "I think my brother is gay." I felt like I would cry myself but managed to hold together. It pierced my heart to think anyone else might have a homosexual family member like I did. Somehow, a calm came over me; I was calmer than I had been in weeks. I had cried a river at the women's conference and shed many tears over the baby squirrel. I would not be any help to my friend if I fell apart in her presence. Besides, if I fell apart, I would have to explain myself, and I was not ready for that. I knew the time would come when I would have to share my sorrow, but I didn't feel like it was the right time.

I listened intently as she talked about the family gathering they had recently and how her mother greeted her brother and his "friend" with open arms. She could not understand why her mom would allow such a thing in her home, and I agreed with her. I couldn't bear the thought of Benjamin bringing his "friend" home for a visit; the very idea was appalling and made me feel sick to my stomach. We prayed together and asked God to reveal truth and expose lies in the life of her brother. Silently, I prayed the same prayer for Benjamin.

I have since realized that two wrongs don't make a right. Showing disgust or hatred toward a gay person's "friend" only brings confirmation of one point: I am filled with hate and disgust. Just because my son is a practicing homosexual, which in God's eyes is sin, doesn't give me the freedom to commit sin by hating another person. I am supposed to follow Christ's example and show love. Not approval—love. There is a difference.

Since Benjamin was attending the Christian school in another town, and he had showed no interest in getting his driver's license, I was the designated driver for the morning commute. The high school in our community was less than a mile away and took less than five minutes to get there, but the new school was about fifteen miles away with more traffic. So our morning commute allowed us more time to talk. My mission was to draw Benjamin out more on the ride, but most of the time he sat and listened. I wanted to tell him that I felt terrible about his abuse. I wanted to say that it was not his fault and it was not our fault either, but I felt like it was my fault and his dad felt the same way but decided that it might do more harm than good.

Many things crossed my mind that I wanted to say. If only he could deal with the past, he might understand that the abuse and the homosexual desires go hand in hand, like a cause and effect situation. Of course he denied the fact that the abuse had anything to do with his feelings, and I knew there were other factors that had a part in the way he felt about himself. Things like low self esteem and a poor self-image contributed to his feelings of inferiority. He didn't feel masculine, he hated sports, and felt intimidated around his male peers. Once the peers label a child as gay, others join in the painful name-calling of that person. Soon they are convinced they are indeed gay and should embrace their new identity.

If only Benjamin would deal with the baggage from his childhood. I understood that dealing with the past could be painful; he would have to relive the events and try to process his pain that occurred, but he said it was no big deal, he had "gotten over it" and just wanted to move on. But it is a big deal—emotionally, physically, and mentally. There are scars left behind when we experience traumatic events that remind us of the ordeal we have endured. Benjamin simply didn't want to admit it; it was easier to say he was over it than deal with it. It's much easier to say, "I was born this way, and the abuse thing has nothing to do with anything." My son was in denial. I could see the pain on his face and in his eyes; there was indeed a battle raging within him. So much for encouraging conversation on our morning commute.

During another of our conversational outings, Benjamin told me of a dream he had. In the dream, he saw a tree in our backyard with black bats hanging all over it. A ladder was propped against the tree and Mike was at the top of it; the girls and I were a few steps below and Benjamin was at the bottom. In his dream, Mike plucked the bats off the tree and handed them down to us, where one of us dipped the bats in batter and passed them over to, you guessed it, Benjamin, and he threw them into the waiting, hot frying pan. What could this possibly mean? Our family took turns analyzing the dream and this is what we came up with. Anna said the tree symbolized Benjamin's life and the bats were "problems" or "unresolved issues." We each helped him get rid of the "problems," and then Benjamin turned them into something good—deep fried, golden bats, to help him grow big and strong. This interpretation sounded a bit weird to me, and I then decided the lot of us had bats in our heads. I wonder what Benjamin's counselor would think.

Another dream he had was even more disturbing. One morning he awoke to find a bald spot on his head that continued to grow. He couldn't understand why his hair was falling out, but I said it was a sign of stress. Maybe he was so stressed that he wanted to pull his hair out. I could certainly relate.

Soon after the strange dreams ceased, a couple of girls from school called and asked Benjamin if he wanted to go hang out at the mall one Sunday afternoon. Having nothing to do at home, he agreed to go along. They were gone a couple of hours and when he returned, he had bought a pair of disgusting jeans. They looked like they had been dragged behind a four-wheeler for about ten miles. He also purchased a pair of strange boxer shorts, which he conveniently forgot to tell me about until I found them in the wash. The waistband had skulls and crossbones all around it, and they were gray and black, definitely foreboding colors. Some time later, I found them in the wash and when I saw them, I screamed out to myself, "What in the heck is this! What does this mean? Is there a hidden message to the boxers, like an obsession with death, dying, or suicide?" I was worked up big time and confronted Benjamin about it. Asking him what it all meant, he laughed at me and said there was no underlying message to the boxers, he just thought they were funny. Yeah, right.

The next day I awoke in grieving mode. I really don't know what triggered the grief; maybe it was the boxers. I was in a very deep pit of funk. I felt like someone I loved very much kept dying-over and over. The number one question kept circling around my brain. "Who is this person living in my precious son's body?" Occasionally I could see glimpses of him, but I didn't feel like I knew him. I didn't know what to say to him; I wanted to hug him, but he acted uncomfortable when I approached him. So we avoided physical contact—no hugging, kissing, or touching. I was worried if I didn't hug him, he would feel badly, but I didn't know what to do. The tension was so strong; the whole family could feel it. A vicious cycle prevailed; what should I say, what should I do, when will it end, will it ever end? What a headache I would get! I felt like I was going insane with the worry. I wondered if Benjamin would come out of this on the other side, healed and whole, or would he slip into the dark world of homosexuality, never to be seen again.

Would he ever find his soul mate, his kindred spirit, who knows his thoughts even while he is thinking them and some day become the proud father of a newborn son or daughter? Or will he one day die of AIDS, sad and alone, disillusioned and disappointed of the life he has lived? Alone, except for his dad and me, and we will never leave him—never. Nothing will ever make us stop loving him.

The Miracle of Christmas

....

Depression continued. I was so sick and tired of feeling sick and tired. A few people at church continued asking me if I felt all right. Once, a friend came up to me and said I looked like I needed a hug. Don't you hate that? I didn't need a hug; I needed a heart transplant because mine was dying. In my mind I wished I were the Tin Man in *Oz*, excitedly waiting to reach my destination; the Emerald City. After the Wizard granted my wish for a brain, he would give me a new heart too. In desperation, I cried out to no one, "Where the heck is that Emerald City and the stupid wizard!"

Really, my friend meant no harm and was genuinely concerned for me, for which I was grateful. I did appreciate her attempt to reach out to me, but I could not explain my appearance. It is unusual for church members to notice when one of the minister's family members looks distraught, because they have their own problems.

It was very difficult to smile and say everything was fine. Of course, a small percentage of people knew I was lying, because I have never been able to hide my emotions very well. One look at my face and anyone would know something was not all right. I should have hung a sign around my neck that said, "Caution: wayward son, depressed mother." I needed a hug, my eye. I needed a sedative, a Prozac, or some other mind-altering drug. One moment I thought I was doing better and *wham*, out of nowhere, I felt like someone was slapping my face, saying, "Wake up stupid! This is reality! Get used to it!" My nerves were shot, my stomach hurt, and I constantly felt like I would throw up. I couldn't sleep, my back hurt constantly, and my neck felt tense and stiff. My insides were gnawing at each other and my nerves felt like they were on the outside of my body. Every noise, no matter how big or small, made me flinch. Just the other day, someone sat at the table reading and started tapping their fingers over and over on the table. *Tap, tap, tap, tap, tap, tap.* What seemed like innocent behavior sent me into a rage. I screamed, "Stop that tapping if you want to keep those fingers!"

My throat kept closing up and I was extremely claustrophobic. I'm sure the general public would have pitied me had they known the trial we were in, and I feel certain some people whispered, "Boy, she looks rough; she could snag lightning and run thunder in a hole." But I didn't care what they thought. I knew what I looked like, and frankly, I didn't care. I was, however, afraid of what might happen to me if things didn't improve. Maybe I would explode like those people who are the victims of spontaneous combustion. For some unknown reason, they just go up in flames and there is nothing left but their shoes. I saw a program about it.

I did have some control; if I let myself cry every time I wanted to, I would do nothing but sit around with a box of Kleenex and cry all day. For some strange reason, I lost four pounds without even trying. At last, something positive, but alas, it was short-lived.

The following morning I rose to take Benjamin to school, and while getting ready, I lost one of my contact lens. I couldn't find it anywhere; it probably fell down the sink or in the toilet. I hoped it would not be an indication of what the rest of the day would be like. Later in the day, I went to check the mail. We received a ridiculous letter saying the bank had frozen our home equity loan, "as we had asked." What? We had done no such thing!

Foolishly, I tried to call the mortgage company and had to wait forever to get a human. When I finally was able to speak to a human, he did some checking and said it was a mistake and to just ignore it. What is wrong with people? There I was, all worked up over some computer error. And some people say computers are more reliable than a person. I'll take a "computer with skin on" any day.

Finally, we had our dinner that evening, and while cleaning up the dishes, a bizarre thing happened. I sprayed out the sink, put the hose back in its little hole, and let go of the handle. Unknown to me, the handle got stuck in the "on" position. When I let go of the handle, it sprayed water all over the counter, the floor, and me. It was the perfect ending to a perfect day.

Soon after the kitchen episode, it was time for a visit with Benjamin's counselor, and he asked me to come along with Mike and our son. Mike and Benjamin had been to several sessions together, but I had never met the counselor. *Maybe it would be good for me to go*, I thought, and I complied. When we arrived and exchanged greetings, I started to feel a little less anxious about the session, and we then went into his office. Benjamin sat in the waiting area while we talked. The counselor asked a lot of difficult questions about my feelings regarding Benjamin's past, and what I had thought would help and encourage me, turned into a heartbreaking conversation. It was like opening a fresh wound that would never heal; it would continue to be torn apart by something someone would say or do.

The counselor spoke candidly with us, telling us of the many parents who were dealing with the same issue and how he could put us in contact with some of them if we wanted him to. I did not like the idea of talking to strangers about such a personal issue but said we would pray about it and let him know. I then waited while Mike and Benjamin went in for their session. Soon, they came out and we left the counselor's office and headed in our separate directions. Mike and I took Benjamin to school, and then we both returned to the church. He went to his office and I went to do some volunteer work. We had not been there for more than an hour when Mike came to get me. He said the school had called and said they needed to meet with us immediately. We had no idea what the problem was, so we went to the school right away.

When we arrived at the principal's office, she told us that Benjamin had received a threatening note in his locker and was very upset. She had ordered a lockdown of the school and was interviewing students from his classes and the friends he had made at the school. She questioned each student and inquired what he or she knew about the note, which read, "Watch your back, fag." Mike and I were devastated that such a thing had happened at a Christian school. We thought things would be different there and hoped that Benjamin's feelings of homosexuality would change, but the terrible subject followed us wherever we went. Eventually, a girl said she knew something about the note. She said Benjamin had confided in her and told her that he was gay. Why would he do such a thing? It seemed like he was trying to turn people against him; why would he think that would be a good thing to do? The girl he confided in told other people, and soon kids were going to him and asking if it were true. Why would Benjamin want people to dislike him? Did he think he deserved some form of punishment or did he just want to get out of that school and return to the public school where his friends were?

Mike and I were at a loss for words. The principal assured us she would get to the bottom of the issue. There was nothing else to say or do, so we all left the school and went home. Mike put in a call to the counselor to see if he could shed any light on the events of the day. The counselor said Benjamin told him he hated the new school; he was depressed and in a fragile state. What the heck did that mean—a "fragile state"? He said we might want to reconsider the school move and let him return to the public school where his friends were; he was afraid our son was suicidal. There was nothing to do but pull him out of the school and send him back to the public school. We sat looking at each other in disbelief, not being able to comprehend it all.

The day's revelations had been too much for Mike and me. At bedtime, we hesitated to go to bed because we knew we would sleep badly, if at all. I tossed and turned, tossed and turned; my mind raced with horrible thoughts. My tear ducts would produce no tears, even though I was in severe pain. All night I moaned and groaned. I drifted in and out of a fitful slumber, moaning and groaning. It felt like someone else was doing the moaning, because I had never heard such a sorrowful sound that couldn't be put into words. I knew it was my voice, but it didn't feel like me. I was having another out-of-body experience; I could see myself looking down on this woeful, pitiful person in excruciating pain. Only I didn't feel pain, at least not physical pain, and I soon realized the pain was emotional. It wasn't one of those things one can pinpoint by saying, "It hurts here." The pain came from within my soul, and it could not be extinguished.

It was one of the longest nights of my life and I was glad when morning came. But in the morning we still had to deal with the issue of school and make a decision about whether Benjamin should or shouldn't go. We decided to let Benjamin stay home. In fact, he stayed home for two days. The following day, his class was to chaperone the first and second graders on a trip to see Disney's Monsters on Ice in Atlanta, and Benjamin decided he wanted to go. After talking with him and making sure he was up for the trip, Mike agreed to take him to school. The closer they got to the school, the more uneasy and agitated Benjamin became. Once they pulled into the parking lot, he became sick to his stomach right in the parking lot. Mike brought him back home and nothing was said about what had happened.

Mike and I decided, along with the counselor's advice, to put Benjamin back in the public school. None of us could continue living like we were living. The semester would end soon, and he would return to his old school after Christmas. We were confident that things would be better; they had to.

Over the next two weeks, some strange things happened. On one occasion while at church, Benjamin disappeared from the church and was seen running down the highway. What was he running from or to? On another occasion, he stayed out later than he was supposed to and would not assume responsibility for his actions. He continued to blame someone else for everything that went wrong.

What our son needed to realize and accept was, what he did now was his responsibility. He was not responsible for the sexual abuse he endured, but he was accountable for the decisions he made now. We all make our own choices and can't blame others for the mistakes we make.

December finally arrived, and Benjamin was out for Christmas break. In January, he would return to his old school with his old friends. My husband and I had many concerns, but we had to think of his emotional well-being. We didn't know what would transpire once Benjamin returned to public school, but we both knew he couldn't continue attending the Christian school and be happy. He was extremely excited to be going back to school with his friends, and we prayed that he would graduate without incident or drama.

Christmas has always been my favorite time of the year, but I didn't feel like celebrating. I had no desire to put up a Christmas tree. I knew if I pulled everything down from the attic and rambled through the ornaments, memories of Christmases past would come rushing to my mind. I knew if I held in my hand the salt dough ornaments the kids and I had made, sadness would descend upon my soul. Each ornament had a child's name on the back because he or she had cut the ornament out, painted it, and then wrote their name on the back with a marker. In my mind, I knew I would see the chubby, little fingers of my son as he carefully worked. And I knew I would be saddened by the thoughts of abuse.

I simply could not have the feelings that usually go along with holidays; warm feelings with family just would not come. I was in mourning. All of my clothes were black because that is what mourners wear. Besides, I didn't want to wear perky pink or sunny yellow, because I did not feel perky or sunny. Instead, a dark cloud followed me everywhere I went.

I did manage to go out among the frenzied shoppers, and without even trying, blended in with the madness. Somehow I got the necessary things done, and when I returned home, tired and grumpy, I was amazed to find that my sweet Beka had climbed into the attic, pulled everything down, and put up the Christmas tree by herself. There it stood—beautiful and bright. I wanted to cry but hugged her instead. It was her way of saying, "I love you mom, and I did this just for you." Isn't it wonderful when we feel like we are alone in the darkness, that someone reaches out to us and warms our heart, letting us know that we are loved?

Magically, my strength was renewed and my courage was bolstered. Christmas truly is a time of miracles.

Let the Healing Begin

....

Who are these people and why do they keep calling our house for Benjamin? One boy in particular called quite often but would never leave a name or number, he would only mysteriously say, "Just tell him I called; he knows who I am." Who is this person? Is there something going on I don't want to know about? Benjamin was becoming more and more secretive and insisted he have his privacy. I wanted to know what was going on in his life but was afraid. You know the old saying, "Ask me no questions, and I'll tell you no lies."

Benjamin has always gotten lots of phone calls from girls. Most of his friends were girls, but something different had started happening. It was all so mysterious. We decided we might need to intervene in some way, so we chose a *Love Won Out* conference that was to be held in February. Mike learned about it while visiting the *Focus on the Family* website. The conference is geared for people who are struggling with same sex attraction, those living a homosexual lifestyle and want to get out, or for those who have a loved one living that lifestyle and need information and help in dealing with the situation. It was in another state and would require two days to allow for travel there and back. When my husband asked him to go, surprisingly, Benjamin agreed to go.

Christmas grew nearer, and I realized the necessity of re-entering the madness outside my home known as the local mall. Anna and Beka decided misery loves company, so they agreed to go along. I had made up my mind that we were going to have fun whether we liked it or not, so off we went. I was concerned that we might have the appearance of three people who had recently escaped an institution where they put people like us, but no one realized that we were not normal, because they were too busy pushing other people out of their way to get the last $9.99 CD player with headphones on the shelf.

Unbelievably, we accomplished quite a bit. I did feel strange while shopping for Benjamin. It felt like I was buying clothes for a dead person, because I felt like he was not really with us, not really dead, just gone somewhere. The body was there but it didn't seem like Benjamin was in the body. The person in his body was a distorted image of what God had created. Daily, I prayed the real Benjamin would return.

Sometimes, I felt very angry around my son. He had hurt me so much, even though I know it was not intentional. He was trying to sort things out in his mind and process what we were saying to him. Still, the harsh words and attitudes hurt me deeply. I heard once that hurting people hurt other people, and I suppose it's true. We do seem to hurt those closest to us, perhaps because we know there is unconditional love between us, and we are always willing to forgive.

The friend I mentioned earlier who thought her brother was gay had found out he really is gay. He had a live-in lover. My friend had to spend Thanksgiving with her family, including her brother and his "friend." She said her family never asked her brother any questions, they just pretended he and his lover were just buddies, and welcome and hug each one when they come to visit. I honestly don't know how I would respond to such an occasion, but I do know if I reject Benjamin's "friend," it will prove detrimental to him and also wound our relationship. I love my son and wouldn't do anything to hurt him, but it would prove extremely difficult for me to do as my friend's mother has chosen to do.

As I thought about my friend's mother, I felt a strong sense of admiration for her. I wondered if she truly had her head stuck in the sand or if she was wiser than my friend thought. Perhaps she had concluded that she could either accept them and see her son, or she could reject them and possibly not have any contact with her son at all. In my opinion, she is much wiser than some might think.

Some days, I have felt very burdened to pray for Benjamin many times throughout the day. Maybe he was about to do something that might harm him or cause him pain, or maybe he was in danger. I don't know and might never know, but when prompted by the Holy Spirit to pray for my son, I do it. I don't have to understand, I leave that up to God. Some things are better left unknown, and sometimes we know things we wish we didn't.

Things like lying. We were disappointed when we found out that Benjamin had been telling us lies. The subject of lying has been discussed at length throughout his childhood, and we repeatedly assured him he would be better off to tell the truth first than wait until later. Besides, somehow we seemed to find out the truth whether he told us or not. Whatever trespass he had committed had to be addressed and have consequences, but if he had lied about it, the punishment would be two-fold; one for the violation and two for the lie. Benjamin could never understand this concept and had a difficult time telling the difference between the truth and a lie. When we caught him in a lie, he would act so offended that we could think that he had lied and yell things like, "You just don't believe me, why don't you ever believe anything I say?" Well, that is fairly simple to explain. Over time, a parent and a child build trust between each other, and when the child lies, the trust is broken and has to be rebuilt. Trust is something you earn, and when it is abused, it becomes difficult to trust again.

Benjamin couldn't get it. Things would go along for a while, and he would answer truthfully about things we asked him. Then out of nowhere, we would catch him in a lie. We wanted to believe him, but he had abused our trust. Sometimes we extended mercy, and sometimes we just didn't feel like being merciful. I'm not sure how my husband felt, but I felt like Benjamin was controlling me emotionally; I felt used. He was definitely jerking my chain. Mike and I struggled in knowing what we should do as far as discipline because we did fear we might do more emotional harm. What is a parent to do? There are no clear-cut answers to such dilemmas; only confusion. We continued to stumble along in the dark.

Christmas finally ended, and the time for Benjamin to return to his old school came. He immediately became comfortable in his surroundings and at ease with his friends because homosexuality is widely accepted in the public school system. Life seemed to settle down. Benjamin baked a chocolate cake for my birthday in early January, and all was right with the world.

One evening, as I read the newspaper, I came across a disturbing article about the gay community. The article said that *Viagra* is a big hit with gay men and often they mix it with *Ecstasy*, for a super sexual high. I wondered why someone would need drugs to be sexually fulfilled. God created us as sexual beings, and sex within marriage is a gift from God meant to be enjoyed and is the ultimate way to express love for each other.

Benjamin had been deceived into thinking that there was a "special someone" out there somewhere waiting for him; that he could have a relationship akin to a heterosexual relationship that would be just as fulfilling. I have read articles about gay couples who have been monogamous for many years but I couldn't help but wonder if that was the exception rather than the rule. I believe that when a man does not and can not meet the emotional needs of another man, he soon seeks out another, hoping this one can fill the void he has in his heart.

Wednesday came, and it was time for the midweek activities at church—Bible study classes, youth get-together, and Awana for the little kids. I had not been there ten minutes when a friend walked up and said she saw Benjamin and another boy leave the parking lot in the other boy's car. I didn't dare think about where they were going and what they might be doing. I knew it couldn't be good if he was skipping church. Our son didn't have a cell phone at that time, so I simply had to wait until they returned.

When church was over, he strolled up like nothing was wrong. "Where have you been?" his dad and I asked him. "I've been helping out in Awana with game time," he said. Naturally, we knew this was fiction and had it on good authority he was nowhere near Awana or anything else that was going on at church. When we told him we knew he and another boy had left the church grounds, he said they never left the church; they only sat in the parking lot talking. About that time, Benjamin's friend, who we found out later was gay, rounded the corner and walked right into our little interrogation. The young man was a terrible liar, and it didn't take long for him to confess. They went and hung out with some friends.

For the next couple of weeks, Benjamin had the pleasure of attending his dad's Bible study class so he could keep an eye on him. It was disturbing to me that we had to constantly watch our son, like a prisoner on a work detail. What else can a parent do with a seventeen-year-old? I cleverly suggested we check into those little ankle bracelets that people have to wear while on house arrest. At least we would have a heads up if Benjamin got the urge to go visiting again.

The date for the *Love Won Out* conference finally arrived in late February. Knowing they had about a five hour drive, Mike planned to leave in time to attend a one night meeting the evening prior to the conference on Saturday, to hear a man who ministers to teenagers. With their bags packed and in the car and good-byes said, they were off for the conference. They arrived in time to hear the speaker, and the information he gave was quite enlightening. In his message, he reprimanded pastors who often insult homosexuals from the pulpit by calling them crude names and showing disgust for their lifestyle. He said that they should be ashamed of their behavior because some parent is sitting in their congregation, weeping over a son or daughter, and that parent needs encouragement instead of insults. Parents are devastated enough without adding insult to injury.

Why do people say things to hurt other people? As Christians, we are guilty of shooting our own wounded, when we should be binding their wounds and trying to lift them up. Just because we show a little love and compassion to someone who is living an alternative lifestyle doesn't mean we agree with their behavior. Jesus, on many occasions, modeled the love we should have for others, especially those who have gotten lost along the way. As the saying goes, "If not for the grace of God, so go we."

The conference, which lasted two days, was extremely informative. But many people who had left the gay lifestyle were not Christians while living the homosexual lifestyle but responded to the gospel when it was shared with them. What about people who have been in church all of their lives, people who have accepted Jesus Christ as their Lord and Savior? Could it be possible to be a Christian and still have same sex desires? Can a person who knows Jesus in an intimate way live a gay lifestyle and not feel any guilt?

In my heart, I believe the answers to these questions are as complex as the reasons and causes of homosexuality. So many people think there is only one reason for living in such a way. If the offending person would just accept Jesus into their heart, everything would be all right. I used to feel the same way, but now I don't have all the answers. It is possible for a Christian, someone who has a relationship with the Lord, to commit other sins, for example, murder and adultery. David was a man after God's own heart, yet he was guilty of both. He committed adultery with Bathsheba and then had her husband placed in the forefront of the battle so he would be killed, enabling him to take Bathsheba as his wife, thus avoiding scandal. Sounds like murder to me.

Even though David committed a great sin, his relationship with the Lord was restored when he confessed his guilt to him and asked for forgiveness. Homosexuality is no different than murder or adultery in God's eyes, yet people look at it differently. I realize the consequences of some sins are greater than others, but they are still sin.

I listened to an awesome speaker the other day on the radio and felt somewhat relieved. The speaker said in hard situations it is our responsibility to do all we can to help in the situation. When we feel like we have done all that we can in our own power, we should ask God if there is anything else we can do. We should then wait on God for the answer and if he tells us we have done everything in our power we could possibly do, then we need to relinquish control and get out of God's way and let him be in control. Sometimes we have to stop doing what we think needs to be done, so God can do what really needs to be done.

When we have done all we could do, then rest in peace, knowing we did all we could. We should exhaust all possibilities as long as they exist and as long as the other person is willing to listen to us. It is a scary thing to say, "All right, God, I'm done. Take over." For some reason we think we know more than God, or at least we act that way. Why are we so reluctant to let God have control? He is God; he knows more than we do, is infinitely more capable than we, yet we still hesitate to give complete control to him. Why do we fool ourselves into thinking we can fix anything? I know I can't fix our problem; only God can *if* Benjamin is willing.

God's grace never ceases to amaze me; he is at work even when we don't realize it. I firmly believe God is at work in not only Benjamin's heart but in ours as well.

Many months ago a fellow church member gave Mike a tape on homosexuality. My husband counsels with people on various topics, and the friend thought that in the course of his counseling, the tape might be valuable to him. At that time, we had no knowledge of Benjamin's abuse, and I firmly believe that God impressed on that person, for reasons unknown to them, to pass it along to Mike. It has helped me tremendously more than the speaker will ever know. The speaker had miraculously emerged unscathed after living in the gay community for many years. He said that when a person realizes someone they love is gay, it triggers a cycle of grief, much like what we enter at someone's death.

After learning that there are stages of grief, I decided to do a little research on the Internet and discovered that there are many sites dealing with the five stages of grief. One such site, *modernlife.org,* tells that in 1969, Dr. Elisabeth Kubler-Ross described in detail the five stages of grief which are: denial, anger, bargaining, depression, and acceptance, in a book titled *On Death and Dying.* According to Kubler-Ross, when we experience the death of a loved one or a similar tragedy, we need to grieve. It is a natural process. It is extremely difficult to deal with the feelings we have and the loss we are faced with in a heartbreaking situation if we fail to grieve.

During the grief process, individuals pass through different cycles in various ways. Some people may take longer in a given cycle than others; some may linger in the cycle of denial, while another person may take longer in the anger phase. Some people may skip some steps altogether and move onto the next phase.

While listening to the tape, I realized what I had been feeling was a normal reaction to the circumstances we were in.

The first thing I experienced was shock (or denial). *This can't be happening to me, there has to be a mistake,* I thought. I proceeded to camp out in this phase with feelings of numbness and being frozen in time. I became deathly ill, unable to function, and the thought of lovemaking with my husband made me feel sick to my stomach. When I thought about sex, the only thing that came to my mind was a sick, perverted mental picture of something that was supposed to be a gift from God to be shared between a married man and woman. I couldn't comprehend the thought of sexual abuse invading our family. We were Christian parents who monitored our children closely. How could this happen? I felt dead inside and wasn't completely sure that was a bad thing. If you're dead, you don't feel pain.

Denial soon gave way to anger. I screamed out to God, "How could you let this happen, God? Where were you when this was taking place? Why didn't you stop this from happening?" I was so hurt that God would let such a thing happen to us; we were serving him sacrificially, and he let this awful thing happen anyway.

Then came the outpouring of tears. I went to bed crying and woke up crying. I cried until I didn't think I could cry anymore, only to be moved to tears by some sappy commercial on television about a mom giving her child a glass of juice and receiving a big hug from her child. Magazines, greeting cards, and touch-feely chick movies made me squall. Unmercifully, the thought tore through my mind, *Where is my hug from my not-so-little boy?* Anger, grief, and panic teamed up to drive me to distraction. I was mad at God, mad at Benjamin's abuser, mad at the world.

I remained in this vicious cycle for over a year. Panic attacks, sleepless nights, and nightmares when I did sleep invaded my life. One of the worst dreams that plagued me was of Benjamin as a small boy and myself walking outside somewhere, maybe a park, enjoying the beautiful sunshine and laughing together. For some reason, I turned my back for what seemed like a mere second in time, and turned back around just in time to see a car driving away with my son looking out the back window. There was the look of terror on his face, and he was crying with his arms outstretched in my direction. I ran after the car as far as I could, but it seemed like my feet were weighted down with something so heavy I could barely pick them up and down. The tag number on the car was a blur, and I couldn't describe the car because my mind just would not remember the color or description. I stood there staring, watching the vehicle go farther and farther away until it disappeared completely.

I woke in a panic and felt like my heart would beat out of my chest. On more than one occasion after having such disturbing dreams, I would jump from bed and run to Benjamin's room, only to find him sleeping soundly like a baby. Relieved, I would return to bed and lay for hours, trying to get the dream out of my head, only to see the image of my little boy crying and reaching out to me every time I closed my eyes.

When I realized protesting in anger was doing no good, I became overwhelmed with hopelessness. Is there any hope for the hopeless? If there is, why do they call it hopelessness? I mean, if the thought of having my son healed and whole again is hopeless, what is a mother to do? I soon realized that the hopelessness wasn't only about Benjamin; it was also about me. I was the hopeless one. I certainly felt hopeless. I didn't care about anything. It didn't matter if it was important or not. I just sat around crying. The tears had decreased to some degree; there would be periods when the crying seemed a thing of the past, and then out of nowhere I would start to weep and not know what had triggered it. Driving was especially difficult, because as I drove, unsettling thoughts would run through my mind.

You know how it is—when you are alone in the car, you can concentrate on matters of importance because you're sitting still and quiet. Many folks do their best thinking while driving because there are few distractions unless you are on the interstate, and then you have to concentrate on traffic. Rarely finding myself on busy highways but on back roads, driving seemed to draw out painful memories. I would vacillate between crying and feeling hopeless, to "I think I feel better. God is in control!" I found myself saying, "I wish I could turn back the hands of time and none of this would have ever happened." I felt so alone and wished there was someone I could run to, who would tell me everything was going to be all right.

Most days during the hopeless and depressed stage, I didn't get dressed until noon. I really had to push myself to shower, dress, and put on a little makeup. I wore a lot of black during that time; almost everything I owned was black. It is the color one should wear to a funeral to symbolize the grieving mode. And I was definitely grieving. Wearing black comforted me somewhat because it had a camouflaging ability that somehow made objects appear smaller that they were. I could grieve and look smaller doing it.

I didn't want to go out in public because I might see someone I knew and they might ask me what was wrong. Especially fellow church members had a way of asking, "Are you okay?" and trigger a sob session. I simply couldn't say why I looked horrible; I had to give a faux answer like, "I'm just tired," or "I didn't sleep well last night." By the looks of things, I hadn't slept in weeks, maybe months. I alternated between the two faux answers but didn't hesitate to use more colorful excuses whenever they came to mind. That wouldn't be considered a lie, would it?

It seemed like I would never get better, and I was convinced that I would spend the rest of my life grieving. I might be like the two dogs in Old Yeller; one died and the other grieved itself to death. (Remember, if you're dead, you don't feel anything). What seemed like eternity but was really the passing of another year, I found myself getting better. Miraculously, I had moved out of the stage of hopelessness and depression and into a phase of hopefulness and acceptance. Healing had begun, and the realization that I couldn't change things but God could seemed to encourage and free me. I had spent two years worrying and fretting over something I could do nothing about.

I had to accept the fact that Benjamin might never change, but I had made the decision to love him anyway. He is my child; nothing can ever make me stop loving him. My love for my son is unconditional; it is not based on his performance or the lack thereof, his lifestyle, or sexual preference. No, I don't agree with his choices, and he knows it. There are some things I won't tolerate, but I will never turn my back on him, disown him, or say mean or hateful things to him or about him. He is a part of me, and I am a part of him. Every chance I get, if he will let me, I tell him how much I love him, hug his neck and kiss his cheek, even if he seems embarrassed. That's what mothers do. We won't rehash the past, but I will tell him I am praying for him.

Life goes on, and I'm just glad Benjamin wants me to be part of his.

Love, not Boot Camp, is the Answer

In March of 2004, there was a lot being said about gays and lesbians and whether they should be able to marry and have their union legally recognized. Every time I turned on the television or radio, the subject was being discussed. Every newspaper, magazine, and newscast had something to say about it. The topic came up during Bible study one evening, and there were some pretty hateful remarks made in my presence. How could the people in my class know this was a super sensitive subject for me? I wanted to get up and leave the room but thought it best to just sit there and wait until the bashing ended. The comments hurt me deeply because they were referring to someone I loved. I can remember making such comments myself, though it seemed like in another lifetime. I wondered how many people I had hurt because of it.

The next day I went to get my roots done. I always feel better after banishing the gray. Later that evening, our senior pastor called my husband and told him that his wife had run into one of our church members who was a teacher at the high school Benjamin attended. She was disturbed because one of her students told her that Benjamin was telling people that he was gay, and she was deeply concerned. We had no choice but to call her and tell her that it was true and to ask for her prayers. The fear that we had dreaded was becoming reality. If Benjamin was telling other kids, soon some parents would know too. Eventually, word would spread and spill over into our church family. What could we do? Would Mike be forced to resign from his position at the church? Would fellow church members snub us or abuse our son verbally? Where would we go and how would we pay our bills?

In desperation, I called a ministry that specialized in homosexuality for guidance and was told by a counselor that since Benjamin would be eighteen in six months, we had very little time to act. She said we should send him to a treatment center for "intense therapy" and gave me a number of such a place thousands of miles away. I called the number and got an answering machine, for which I was glad. I didn't feel right about sending our son across the nation for "intense therapy" and was more than a bit disturbed by such terminology. What kind of place was this? What kinds of methods did they use? The whole thing gave me the creeps. I love my son too much to do such a thing. I couldn't help him by sending him away from everything and everyone he knew.

At church that Wednesday evening, a friend came and got me from my class to tell me that no one knew Benjamin's whereabouts. He should have been with the youth but wasn't there. The friend said he had seen him briefly, but when he turned around, Benjamin was gone. My heart started racing wildly, and mentally, I imagined all sorts of things happening. Where in the world could he be? Things had settled down to some degree, and he hadn't tried to sneak off in quite some time. After a few tense minutes, Benjamin was located. He was indeed still on the church campus helping a teacher with a class of preschool-

ers. After the previous disappearance, the youth leaders
had begun watching him more closely. He simply slipped
out and no one saw where he went. He was innocent of
any wrongdoing, except leaving his group without telling
someone, and was offended that people were scouring the
earth for him.

He had really gotten himself into a mess. He had
become somewhat of an outcast in the youth group, because
the kids didn't know what to say to him, so they didn't say
anything. He had one friend, a girl, that had been his friend
for years, and she has remained a faithful friend to this day.
The youth leaders, however, were having a difficult time
knowing what to do or say and didn't appreciate his open-
ness with the kids in the group. One leader told him he was
poisoning the youth group; rejection by his peers quickly
followed.

There were nagging questions in my and Mike's mind.
Why had Benjamin not come to us about the abuse sooner?
He said that he did say something about it when he was
around nine years old, but we didn't do anything about it.
We did remember the conversation but our recollection
was somewhat different than his. He did say that Derek
had touched him in a place he shouldn't have, but after
further questioning, Benjamin said it had only happened
once. Mike assured him he was not in trouble in any way
and wanted to make sure there wasn't more to it since he
couldn't seem to get the incident out of his mind. He said
that was all that happened, but he felt badly about it. Why
had he not told the complete truth? Was he embarrassed
to tell? Did Derek threaten him in some way? Benjamin
said no to all of the above questions, but said he was afraid
to tell everything, so he walked around for roughly eight

years feeling guilty and battling the feelings he had about the incident. It broke my heart to think that he carried the guilt that long, not knowing what to do or where to turn. He said he felt better about it after getting assurance of his relationship with the Lord in the eighth grade, but the old feelings, the same sex attraction, invaded his thoughts once again. He said he just got tired of fighting the feelings and decided to give in to the desire.

He felt accepted at school, and his friends encouraged him to be who he really was. Both Mike and I apologized for not investigating further into the comments he had made at age nine and asked for forgiveness. How could we have been so stupid? We had a productive talk and were beginning to understand how Benjamin felt. He was very relieved that we were not sending him back to the Christian school or to some "spiritual boot camp" he had heard about. I told him it had indeed crossed our minds, but we loved him too much to do such a thing. The fear of never seeing my son terrified me. I firmly believe had we sent our son away, when upon turning eighteen, he would have run away and kept on running as far as he could get from us and we would never see him again. He didn't need a boot camp; he needed our unconditional love, and we made sure he got it.

If only Benjamin accepted the fact that sexual abuse at an early age had a profound effect on his mind and desires. If only he would realize that and try to deal with the baggage that goes along with sexual abuse, he might see things differently. But he didn't want to admit that sexual abuse and homosexual feelings were somehow connected.

Everywhere I go and everyone I talk to seems to have a gay or lesbian issue. At church one Sunday, I went to pray with a friend at the altar and found out she has a lesbian sister who wants to "come out." She was very burdened for her sister, and the extended family was not pleased with her because she wouldn't condone her sister's choice. Because my friend is a Christian, she endured criticism for her beliefs. I've also learned of other brothers and sisters in Christ who were dealing with similar problems. Since learning of Benjamin's decision to live a gay lifestyle, we have continued to hear of sons, daughters, and wives who have walked away from their former lives to enter the gay community. The families left behind, who are trying to pick up the pieces of a life they once knew, need support from those who have made the journey and are successfully dealing with the issues associated with a homosexual family member. Why are there no support groups available for grieving moms and dads? I wanted to help, but didn't know what to do.

I hesitated to give others advice, because I fell into that trap long ago, giving unsolicited advice on such topics as child-rearing, marriage, and any other family issues and inflating my ego as I went along. Pride is such a destructive force; it quietly creeps in unaware, and soon we are quite convinced we know all there is to know about everything. Compliments and praise feed the pride growing in us. Some people just can't handle praise, as it goes right to their head and becomes blown out of proportion. Soon they are praising themselves.

Jesus never exalted himself above others but was the perfect example of humility. David, a man after God's own heart, thought he was above correction, and his arrogance got him into a lot of trouble. He let pride take control of his thoughts and then committed adultery and murder and convinced himself that no one had authority over him. Besides, he was the king and he made all the rules. But God was not pleased with David and he paid the price for the sin he committed by losing the child conceived with Bathsheba.

Why, oh why, do we ignore the pleading of the Holy Spirit? He urges us to deal with our issues and be free from them, but we continue dragging them behind us like a ball and chain. Sometimes we don't realize we have baggage because we have carried it around for so long, and it feels natural to have it with us. Everybody has problems, and it is just a way of life. Job said that man born of woman is of few days and full of trouble (Job 14:1 NIV). But that doesn't mean we should be content with the baggage, especially when God has made a way to rid ourselves of it. Many times we drag our issues around behind us, thinking, *Poor me, I have so much baggage, everybody should feel sorry for me.* And we live for the sympathy that others extend to us when God's word says that we can know the truth and the truth will set us free—free from the self-pity, the pain, the shame, and the bitterness; free from the guilt, deception, arrogance, and prejudice.

Our mind is a powerful thing, and all sin is conceived in the mind. When we think about things we shouldn't, our mind can influence us to act on our thoughts and then the thoughts bring forth sin. Our heart is also deceptive and desperately wicked (Jeremiah 17:9 KJV), convincing us we have a right to be happy, and we should do whatever it is that makes us happy regardless of who we might hurt along the way. But we should not compare our self with other people and what they have or what they do. We are to compare our self with Christ and him alone. He is our example, and we must submit our will to him daily.

How can we deal with our stuff when we won't let Jesus into the secret places of our mind and heart? We must allow and not only allow but invite him into the clandestine corners where our hidden transgressions and indiscretions are securely stashed away. Jesus will never push his way in because he is the perfect gentleman, and he patiently waits for us to ask him in. Once admitted, he will lovingly and gently deal with each piece of baggage we have and sadly look upon the distasteful fragments left behind and lovingly say, "I died for this, I came to heal these wounds, I can restore you and put the pieces of your life back together, but you must be ready to surrender everything, and I mean everything, to me."

Not only do we have to surrender our baggage to Jesus in order to have healing from painful experiences, we have to be willing to forgive the abuser and surrender the anger and bitterness we may have to God. If we feel abandoned by God and want to blame him for our troubles, we must also surrender those feelings if we expect full restoration. It is true that, in the life of a believer, God either allows or directs events into our lives. I also know that things happen as a result of sin and the fallen condition of man. Sometimes, people inflict pain on others that don't deserve the pain.

Bad things happen to good people, and good things happen to bad people; it rains on the just and the unjust (Matthew 5:45 KJV). What truly matters is what we do with the painful events that come into our lives. We can become angry and blame God, or we can trust God to tell us what we can learn from the situation. In the life of a Christian,

God can make something good from the bad things in life. When we wait patiently before God, in time he will bind up the brokenness, restore body, soul, and mind; he can take the shattered pieces of a person's life and make it into something that will bring him glory. The choice is ours.

In late March of 2004, God impressed upon me to pray for Benjamin's protection from Satan. The seducer, the liar, and the father of all lies, the destroyer would love nothing better than the destruction of my son. I believe Benjamin knows the Lord and Satan knows he cannot have his soul, but he can infiltrate his mind with thoughts of helplessness and defeat. I can imagine him saying to Benjamin, "It's useless, you'll never change. The gay lifestyle is your destiny, besides, your parents will never accept you because you can never please them. Why don't you just give up? You'll never win; just end it all and you won't feel the pain anymore." Satan knows he can't have my son's soul, but he can make his life miserable, so much so, that he may take his own life.

I prayed for him for a long time, and I felt God urging me to anoint Benjamin's room with oil. I felt really strange doing it, but I had to do whatever I could to protect him from the destroyer. I anointed the outside of the door and the headboard of his bed. An eerie feeling filled the room, and I felt like I was not alone. I don't to this day know what was going on in our son's life at that time, but I feel confident there was a battle raging that only God could see, and he intervened on his behalf.

The next day was an especially stressful day, and I felt that maybe Satan was out for revenge for yesterday. I woke up feeling down, and first thing, I burned my toast, my grits boiled over in the microwave, and I burned my finger and forehead with the curling iron. See what I mean? Burnt toast, burnt skin—it had to be Satan.

But soon, Mike and I would attend the Minister of Education conference, a learning retreat for ministers of education and their wives. We both looked forward to the annual event with excitement and expectation and were thankful for some time away. I am so glad I went as I almost backed out of going at the last minute with all the major hoopla that was going on. It was held at a beautiful mountain resort, and our room had a fireplace! We were surrounded with gorgeous scenery, our meals were elegantly catered throughout the conference, and just being away from home calmed us both. The conference had special sessions for the wives of the ministers, and we played games to get acquainted with each other. Many of the women had attended for several years, and they enjoyed visiting and talking with friends from past years.

One lady in particular, whom I've never met, shared with the group about her eleven-year-old son who had a lot of problems and was seeing a psychiatrist because he was suicidal. He was on Zoloft and for some reason was very angry. I couldn't believe my ears, I felt like I were she. After the session was over, I talked with her at length about her son and encouraged her to sit down with him when she returned home and ask some difficult questions. His behavior made me think of Benjamin and the anger he exhibited while in middle school. I realize every person who is angry and on medication has not been sexually abused, as there are many different causes for depression and anger issues. We prayed together, and as I left, I felt the sorrow of that mother and the feeling of helplessness that she expressed. I sincerely hope her son is not a victim of any type of abuse—sexual or otherwise. I am, however, beginning to realize sexual abuse is a far greater problem than we might ever know.

After returning from the conference, life continued on its somewhat abnormal path. Mornings were especially difficult for me for unknown reasons. Some days I thought I couldn't go on anymore. Grocery day was something I dreaded terribly. When I went shopping, I felt like I was in the store for hours and would never get out alive. It seemed like they put things in a certain place, and once you learned where everything was, overnight they changed it all around. If they knew what I was dealing with, they would stop this nonsense and leave things alone. One more "reset" and I might just freak out on the produce aisle and start throwing potatoes at the produce guy. I prayed daily that I wouldn't be guilty of such irrational behavior.

God Promises Me a Sound Mind

At the Minister of Education conference, one of the speakers for the wives said that we have to filter every thought that comes into our mind. What comes natural is listening to the thought, dwelling on the thought, believing the thought, and finally, acting on the thought. It we don't try to filter out the negative thoughts, we can get into some pretty big trouble. Suddenly, I realized that was part of my problem. I needed to learn how to expel negative, depressing thoughts. If I didn't, I would never get out of the prison of depression. I had to learn how to guard my mind. The speaker said that she carried index cards with her everywhere, and when she had to wait somewhere, she pulled them out and memorized scripture. What a great idea!

Encouraged, I thought if I could concentrate on positive thoughts instead of the lies of Satan, I might get better! I made the index cards, and they started helping immediately. Every morning I got them out and read each one. It was amazing the difference it made to fill my mind with encouraging scripture each morning instead of sad, gloomy thoughts.

It was now early April of 2004. For some reason, I had been thinking a lot about last summer. What a nightmare! Looking back, I don't know how I lived through it. The whole revelation of the abuse and Benjamin's desire to live an openly gay lifestyle seemed like a very bad dream. I still have bad days, but things are beginning to get better and the bad days are getting farther apart.

As I sat thinking about the loneliness and depression of the past two years, I again, felt completely convinced that a large majority of church members think their pastors are perfect, and that is why some people may hesitate to fellowship with them. And we need fellowship! They are afraid they might say something wrong or that the pastor will analyze every statement or facial expression. If only they could realize that we are people just like they are, and we have problems just like they do. Just because God has called someone to a specific ministry doesn't mean they never have problems. I know people look up to those in ministry as an example of how they should live, but they should be looking to Jesus for guidance instead. People will let us down every time. Only Jesus is our constant.

Some church members think that we are the Cleavers. You know, Wally, the Beaver, June, and Ward; the perfect textbook family. We have lovely dinners with everyone smiling and saying, "Mom, what a tremendous dinner! Is that a new dress? Those pearls look lovely with the dress. That color of green compliments your eyes, and that shade of lipstick is gorgeous!" To which mom replies, "Thank you, children, who is ready for a piece of my blue ribbon, seven layer chocolate cheesecake with only ten grams of fat and 100 calories?"

Oh please, that is pure fiction. Every pastor's wife sometimes serves burned rolls, mystery meat casserole, and flat cakes because someone opened the oven door just when they shouldn't have. Please believe me, I am not June Cleaver! I am plain old me, a normal person just like you, with possibly more problems than you care to hear about.

I have needs just like any other person, needs like having a dear friend I can be myself with, a friend I can tell anything to without condemnation. I need someone who will listen to my troubles and let me cry on her shoulder. I need to be heard and understood and have my feelings validated. I need to have a friend I can run to when I feel like my world is falling apart.

I know that God is my refuge and is ever waiting for me to come to him with all of my cares, but it sure is nice to have a sister in the Lord who can understand.

In a journal entry on April 19, 2004, I read in Psalm 32, that God is my hiding place.

> You are my hiding place; you will protect me from trouble and surround me with songs of deliverance. Selah. I will instruct you and teach you in the way you should go; I will counsel you and watch over you. Psalm 32:7,8 (NIV)

What an interesting analogy; the first thought that came to my mind was one of myself as a child. As kids, we played hide and seek often, and everyone who played wanted the perfect hiding place. I had such a place, the kind that no one could ever find me in. After everyone had been found, I would sneak out slowly so my special place would not be revealed. Game after game, whoever was "it" failed to find me.

Occasionally I did hide in other places and would let whoever was "it" find me, allowing them to think they knew my special spot, even though they didn't. So it is with God. He is my hiding place, and no one can harm me as long as I am hidden in him.

As I sat thinking about childhood games and the comparison of God being my hiding place, I heard some neighbor children playing hide and seek close by. A small voice called out, "1–2–3–4–5–6–7–8–9–10! Ready or not, here I come!" How that took me back, and at the very moment I sat thinking about God being my hiding place. God has a way of showing himself when we least expect it and confirm truth to us.

But to Satan, it is no simple game children play; he plays for keeps. Satan relentlessly searches for you and me and wants to kill, steal, and destroy. But Christ came to give us life and give it more abundantly (John 10:10 KJV). Thank God he is my hiding place and will protect me from trouble and surround me with songs of deliverance (Psalm 32:7 NIV). I will dwell in the shadow of the everlasting arms; he is my fortress and high tower and will draw me into his all-encompassing arms and pull me close to him and there I am safe. He wants to do the same thing in Benjamin's life if he will let him.

I thought of something recently that helped relieve some of the guilt I felt concerning Benjamin's abuse. I thought of God the Father, the most perfect parent there ever was or will be. God the Father has never done anything wrong, nor can he, yet he has many rebellious children. You and I for example. Not only are we rebellious, we constantly mess up, make bad choices, and fail to do what we should. We're pretty good at doing what we shouldn't, and according to Paul, it's forever a struggle to behave.

> I do not understand what I do. For what I want to do I do not do, but what I hate I do. And if I do what I do not want to do, I agree that the law is good. As it is, it is no longer I myself who do it, but it is sin living in me. I know that nothing good

lives in me, that is, in my sinful nature. For I have
the desire to do what is good, but I cannot carry it
out. For what I do is not the good I want to do; no,
the evil I do not want to do-this I keep on doing.
Romans 7:15–19 (NIV)

Yes, God is the perfect parent, and we are his imperfect
children. We will undoubtedly make wrong choices and sin;
God gives us the ability to choose. Many times we choose
the wrong thing, like Paul, but God doesn't stop loving us
when we sin, he loves us with an everlasting love. God the
Father could have made us perfect, but he wanted his children to serve and obey him from a heart of love.

My child is no different. I can't make choices for him,
although at times I wish I could. He makes his own choices
and will deal with the consequences, whatever they may be.
My job as a parent, and yes, it sometimes feels like a job, is
to love my son unconditionally and pray for God to reveal
truth and expose lies. I can love my son but not agree with
his choices; he is still my son, and I will never stop loving
him.

Sometimes, something goes haywire in our brain, and
we don't process information correctly, and we fail to see
things from God's perspective. We only see what we want
and dive headlong into impending disaster. Thank God we
have a heavenly Father who is patient, kind, and longsuffering. He is forever willing to forgive, no matter how many
times we mess up. Shouldn't we, as parents, do the same?
Psalm 103 tells us how compassionate and gracious God
is.

He does not treat us as our sins deserve or repay us
according to our iniquities. For as high as the heav-

ens are above the earth, so great is his love for those who fear him; for he knows how we are formed, he remembers that we are dust. Psalm 103:10,11,14 (NIV)

I know I can trust God for the end result concerning Benjamin and his choices. I don't have to understand to trust; I may never understand why God let the abuse happen to our son, but I will always acknowledge him as God. He is sovereign, mighty, and powerful and nothing is too hard for him. There never has been nor ever will be a god as mighty as he. He created the earth, the heavens, and the seas and everything and everybody in them. Like Peter, I have to ask, "Lord, to whom shall we go? You have the words of eternal life. We believe and know that you are the Holy One of God" (John 6:68 NIV). He is the one. The only one.

There is no other who can help us when we make a mess of our lives. He alone is able to put the pieces back together and make us fit for his use. I have no desire but to take God at his word, for his word is true.

Matthew told a story in chapter twenty-one about a fig tree Jesus spoke to, and it withered before the disciple's eyes, and they couldn't believe how it withered so quickly.

Jesus replied, I tell you the truth, if you have faith and do not doubt, not only can you do what was done to the fig tree, but also you can say to this mountain, 'Go throw yourself into the sea,' and it will be done. If you believe, you will receive whatever you ask for in prayer. Matthew 21:21,22 (NIV)

Of course, I know our request must be in God's will and be consistent with scripture. I know it is God's will for Benjamin to leave the gay lifestyle, which according to scripture is sin, and I know it is not God's will for him to continue in sin. He is a prodigal and God's desire for prodigals is for them to return home. Patiently he waits. Just as the father in the parable of the lost son in Luke 15, God waits.

> When he came to his senses, he said, "How many of my father's hired men have food to spare, and here I am starving to death! I will set out and go back to my father and say to him: Father, I have sinned against heaven and against you. I am no longer worthy to be called your son; make me like one of your hired men." So he got up and went to his father. But while he was still a long way off, his father saw him and was filled with compassion for him; he ran to his son, threw his arms around him and kissed him. The son said to him, Father, I have sinned against heaven and against you. I am no longer worthy to be called your son. But the father said to his servants, "Quick! Bring the best robe and put it on him. Put a ring on his finger and sandals on his feet. Bring the fattened calf and kill it. Let's have a feast and celebrate. For this son of mine was dead and is alive again; he was lost and is found." So they began to celebrate. Luke 15:17–24 (NIV)

God would love nothing better than to see my son coming over the horizon. Even though he may bear the scars of sin, God will stretch out his arms, with tears streaming down his face, and welcome him home.

It is what I live for.

One evening in late July before Benjamin's senior year of high school, two young men I had never seen before walked into church and made a beeline straight for Benjamin. He seemed to know them, and they talked and laughed together before the service started. To my surprise, they both stayed for the service and the three sat together. After the service was over, our son asked if he could go with his friends to grab something to eat, and we said yes. Shortly after they left, a friend who was a teacher at the high school told us that the two boys were gay and were very verbal about their homosexuality. It seemed like Benjamin was mocking us, like he was saying, "This is the way I am, and you can't do anything about it." I found it very disturbing that our son would bring in reinforcements, like it was us against him. It felt like he was taunting us and trying to think of ways to hurt us, and he was being quite successful. He was encouraged by his friends at school to just accept who he was and was told that we were old, intolerant, narrow-minded, and didn't know what we were talking about, basically that we were stupid.

I've lived a lot longer than those little pipsqueaks have, and I've been around the block a few times. I am not stupid. It sounds like to me they are the ones who are not the sharpest tool in the shed. They only know what they've been told by other people. Why do teenagers accept what their peers tell them as truth, while rejecting advice from their parents? It would be common sense to listen to someone who has lived longer and experienced more during their lifetime, but they are convinced that parents couldn't possibly understand. Satan's deception continues.

Why can't Benjamin realize he is being deceived? Why can't he see that a spiritual battle rages in his mind and heart? Satan only seeks to steal, kill, and destroy. He is a liar, the father of all lies, the destroyer and the thief and would love nothing more than to destroy our family, our home, our marriage, and our testimony. Only God prevents it.

A few days after the latest run-in, I had a very disturbing dream. So terrible I dare not even write it down for fear it might come true. In the dream, I cried and cried and woke myself up crying. It was so real, I felt like I was living the dream and couldn't go back to sleep for hours. Every time I tried to go to sleep, the images reappeared in my mind. I prayed desperately for them to stop.

A month passed and God began showing me that he is in control, and I don't have to be. I was so tired of carrying my burden, so tired of worrying, so tired of crying. I was physically exhausted from the emotional overload. I was also tired of the meltdown syndrome I floated in and out of. I knew I had to completely give God my burden, because I just couldn't carry it anymore. God's word says, "For God hath not given us the spirit of fear, but of power, and of love and of a sound mind (2 Timothy 1:7 KJV)." Boy, was that good news! God is going to keep me from losing my mind! I made a conscious decision to no longer live in fear. I no longer would vacillate between wanting to die and being afraid to live.

I want to live.

I Want to Live Again

....

The time finally came for me to start back living my life. I had to think about good things and leave the rest to God. Philippians 4:8 NIV reads,

> Finally, brothers, (or sisters) whatever is true, whatever is noble, whatever is right, whatever is pure, whatever is lovely, whatever is admirable-if anything is excellent or praiseworthy-think about such things.

I knew all along that I could trust God in this and any other crisis, but I was afraid. I was afraid to say to God, "Okay, God, do whatever is necessary to bring Benjamin back to you." When we say such things, it can be terrifying because we don't know exactly what that might include. It might take something bad, and I don't like bad.

If I say, "do whatever," does that mean I don't care what happens? No, I'm saying I trust God even though I don't know what the future holds. Before, I had said "whatever God," but I didn't really mean it. I sort of meant it, and even wanted to believe I meant it, but I just couldn't let go. Why do we think we have to worry when we can do so little about our problems? We can't be everywhere, but God can. We can't hear and see everything, but God can. We don't know what's in a person's heart, but God does.

I can only guess what Benjamin feels in his heart, but God knows what he feels. I can't see inside his mind or understand what he is thinking, but God can. And he can be trusted. I decided I would get out of God's way and stop hindering him, because I had done all I could. I decided to surrender control to him. There is something very liberating about saying that and really meaning it. I can relax— God is on the throne. I am done with battling fear and doubts, swinging back and forth between believing God, not believing God, believing God, not believing God.

The whole believing, not believing thing strangely made me think of one of my favorite movies, *Miracle on 34th Street*. In the movie, little Susan was a very matter-of-fact child who didn't believe in Santa Claus or anything make-believe. She and her mother lived in New York, but Susan yearned for a house in the country—one with a swing in the backyard. Susan met a man who said he was Santa, and he asked her what she wanted for Christmas, and she said a house in the country, not really believing he could get it for her.

Christmas day arrived and Susan didn't get what she had asked for; her mother was right. There was no Santa Claus. But her mother said something totally out of left field; she said to believe anyway, she said that sometimes you have to believe even when it doesn't make sense. Poor Susan kept repeating over and over, "I believe, it doesn't make sense, but I believe." And as you know, if you've seen the movie, Susan's dream of a house with a swing came true.

I had felt the same way for a long time. Like the scripture in Mark chapter 9 that describes a father's son who was possessed by a spirit that seized him and threw him into the fire, Jesus rebuked his disciples for not being able to cast out the spirit saying;

"O unbelieving generation," Jesus replied, "how long shall I stay with you? How long shall I put up with you? Bring the boy to me." So they brought him. When the spirit saw Jesus, it immediately threw the boy into a convulsion. He fell to the ground and rolled around, foaming at the mouth. Jesus asked the boy's father, "How long has he been like this?" "From childhood." He answered, "it has often thrown him into fire or water to kill him. But if you can do anything, take pity on us and help us." Mark 9:19–22 (NIV)

What an unbelievable statement! "'If you can'?" said Jesus. "Everything is possible for him who believes" (verse 23). To which the father replied with a paradoxical statement in verse 24. Immediately the boy's father exclaimed, "I do believe; help me overcome my unbelief!" And God immediately cast out the evil spirit. I too have had doubts concerning Benjamin's future and have cried out to God, "I believe, help my unbelief." And he has increased my faith.

A miraculous thing happens when we choose to believe God; he teaches us very useful and significant life lessons in the "It doesn't make sense, but I believe" stage. While we are waiting, God teaches us perseverance, patience, and hope. We must never give up—all things are possible with Christ. One day soon I pray that Benjamin will feel a strong desire to seek God's will for his life. When he cries out to God and wants answers to questions like, "Who am I? Why am I so confused, who can help me, who can I trust?" God will answer him clearly, "Who are you? You are mine. Why are you so confused? Satan desires to sift you like wheat. Who can help you? I can. I am the great I am, the creator of mankind, and the maker of heaven and earth.

I am the great physician, the balm of Gilead, the tender, loving Savior of your soul. You can trust me.

"I gave everything for you, even my only Son. Your sins are paid for with the shed blood of Jesus Christ. Drop after drop spilled forth, down through the ages of time, flowing like a never-ending river, washing, cleansing, redeeming all who kneel in its path. I did this for you. You are mine and I am yours. You can trust me." Oh, how I pray my son soon realizes that Jesus is waiting for him. He alone has the answers to Benjamin's questions.

By this time, we were well into Benjamin's senior year of high school. Upon finding some questionable material on our computer one afternoon, Mike and I decided to have a talk with Benjamin when he came home from work. He admitted to down loading the pictures on the computer and said he was sorry he had done it.

In the course of the conversation, he said he had decided he didn't believe in God anymore, nor did he believe in Satan. He said he did believe in heaven, somewhere, but didn't believe in hell. He said he was tired of feeling bad about himself and beating himself up about the gay thing. He said when he was younger, he thought if he prayed harder and read his Bible more, the feelings would go away, but they never did. And that is why he didn't believe in God, because he didn't help him with his problem. That was a difficult thing to hear. I asked God to help me understand why his prayer went unanswered, but I didn't get the answer at that time. It did, however, come later.

The next day Benjamin hid out in his room until everyone, except me, left the house. He finally came out and gave me a hug. He said he wanted to make us proud of him and he felt really badly about the pictures on the computer.

I knew he was terribly embarrassed and ashamed of his actions, so I tried to think of things I could say that would encourage him. I told him his dad and I loved him very much and were proud of him. He has so many wonderful qualities.

He is a compassionate person and considerate of others and kind and would give you his last dollar if he thought you needed it. I continued to tell him, while we were disappointed by his actions, we would never stop loving him. Even if he chose to live the gay lifestyle until his dying day, we would love him still and nothing could change our feelings for him. He started to cry, and we hugged for a long time. Unbelievably, I did not cry.

A few days passed, and by a miracle of God, I never cried over the latest discovery. The next day proved to be a strange day for our family. On the way home from class, Beka's car broke down in the middle of the highway and refused to move. By highway, I mean *big* highway. She called me and was screaming and crying into the phone. I knew something terrible must be wrong. She had made her exit when the car died on the exit ramp, and she didn't know what to do. I was concerned for her safety since other cars were exiting too. Strangely, God sent a man in a big cowboy hat to push her to the side of the road so other cars could pass. I managed to calm her down and told her I would get her dad to come and get her.

Complete with tow truck, Mike found her and brought her safely home. Unbelievably, we found out later, a brake pad had fallen off the car, and as a safety precaution, the car refused to go any farther. I was so worked up and in an itchy frame of mind after the phone call from Beka, I launched into a cooking frenzy. I put on a roast, a chicken, and assorted side dishes. I don't know what I was thinking, nothing was ready by suppertime and choir practice that evening. So we had to get take out so my husband could go to church. I, on the other hand, stayed home and monitored the buffet line until it finished cooking and afterward cleaned up the mess.

The next day, I was still reeling from the excitement of the cowboy and the bake-a-thon. I needed a diversion. There were only two things that would calm my fevered brow: One, a trip to Wal-Mart or Big Lots to check out the clearance rack, and two, some comfort food; large fries with lots of catsup and a large sweet tea with lemon! Yum, yum! It tasted wonderful! With renewed courage, I was certain I could face whatever tomorrow might bring. The strange events of the prior day were as good as forgotten.

Late February 2005 rolled around, and it was time to visit my family doctor so I could get new prescriptions on my maintenance drugs—blood pressure medicine and reflux meds. I should have seen the meltdown coming. All the way to the doctor's office I was in a panicky mood. There was such a heavy fog, I thought several times I might have to pull over. Each time I met a car, I felt like I might lose control and crash into someone. Somehow, I managed to make it to the office in one piece. The doctor came in, and I went to pieces right there on the examination table. I started to cry and carry on about kids, fog, and my weight, which unfortunately had markedly increased. The doctor was very kind, and he let me rage on about my problems. When I finished talking, he said he would put our family on his prayer list.

In late March, Benjamin was beginning to get worried about college. He seemed to be stressed about the fact that he would have to share a room with another guy and asked if he could get a private room. The dorm rooms were really large and were suite-style with a bath between the two bedrooms. We really didn't see any way to swing the private room since it was more expensive, and we already had to borrow money for tuition, so we decided a private room wouldn't be an option. Our son brooded over the fact and nervously accepted the truth that he would have to live with someone he did not know. The idea disturbed him greatly.

During his last year of high school, Benjamin worked a lot of hours at the grocery store saving for college. He was plagued with mood swings; he was extremely happy one minute and sad a short time later. The thought of leaving his friends behind and not seeing them on a regular basis was disturbing to him. He would have to start over and make new friends, and the thought unnerved him greatly. Many changes in his life were in store with rooming with someone he had never met before, living in a new place, and finding his way around and having much more freedom than he had ever had.

One month before graduation, our son was irritable and bad-tempered. He occasionally overslept, saying he didn't feel well and didn't want to go to school. After two days of oversleeping, I was losing my patience. After trying to wake him and get him moving, he raised his voice at me and pointed his scrawny finger at me and said, "Don't provoke me!" To which I said, "Don't talk to me like that." To which he said, "I can if I want to, I'm an adult!"

Big mistake.

His dad stepped in and instructed him to apologize, which he did grudgingly. By that time, I was quite steamed and responded to his apology with, "Big whoo!" Things escalated a bit and he said, "What did you say?" I told him to behave, or he would find himself either walking to school or riding the big yellow cheese.

Time flew. Graduation was two weeks away. I wandered around the house thinking what it would be like with Benjamin gone. So much was changing. In less than three months Benjamin would leave for college. How did time pass so quickly? At times I felt excited for him and at other times I felt afraid. I was afraid of the unknown. Would Benjamin adjust to college life? Would he instantly make friends, or would he pine away in loneliness?

These thoughts, among many others, consumed my mind. Though in a strange way I knew I would feel a release once Benjamin was gone. My time of fretting was over; my liberation was very near. I had done my job as a parent the best way I knew how. From then on, Benjamin's future would be in his hands. He would be held accountable for the decisions he made and, quite honestly, I was overjoyed at the prospect of letting go. I could taste freedom.

In what seemed like a blink of an eye, graduation came and Benjamin graduated with honors. As I sat watching him cross the stage to receive his diploma, I felt a deep sense of pride and joy. He had reached a milestone in his life and had done it quite well. My son amazed me, wowed me, and I was proud to be his mother. One door closed and another one opened before him. It would be his decision as to how he would finish. Many prayers were made on his behalf over the next three months.

Late July brought the realization that our son would be leaving in less than a month. God told me that the time for mourning had passed. Even though I had surrendered

Benjamin's future to God, I still mourned for him. I loved him so much and knew I would miss him terribly. Matthew 5:4 NIV says, "Blessed are those who mourn, for they will be comforted." I knew Jesus would comfort me once Benjamin was gone because he had given me the strength to let him go. He also encouraged me with a verse in Jeremiah. "Then maidens will dance and be glad, young men and old as well. I will turn their mourning into gladness; I will give them comfort and joy instead of sorrow" (Jeremiah 31:13 NIV).

I was definitely looking forward to some joy in my life.

I was officially done with sackcloth and ashes; I was finished wearing the grave clothes and made a promise to myself to stop wearing so much black. No fear. God is God. Is there anything too hard for him? No. Did I know what might happen? No. Does God? Yes! Is he in control? Yes! Can he be trusted? Yes!

I have come full circle. God has assured me that I will not lose my mind because he gives me "the spirit of power (not fear), and of love (not hate or disgust), and of a sound mind" (not insanity!) (2 Tim. 1:7 KJV). My heart is healing: "He heals the brokenhearted and binds up their wounds" (Psalm 147:3 NIV), and he has given me courage: "Have I not commanded you? Be strong and courageous. Do not be terrified; do not be discouraged, for the Lord your God will be with you wherever you go" (Joshua 1:9 NIV). What a promise!

I have reached the final stage of the grief process. I accept the fact that Benjamin may never change, but I have an amazing freedom to love him anyway.

The Big Day

The final day before the big day arrived. Benjamin would officially be a college freshman in twenty-four hours! He had his room assignment and had gotten acquainted with his roommate over the phone. On several occasions, they had talked, deciding who would bring what. While Benjamin was on a Wal-Mart run, the roomie called and wanted to speak to him. After telling him Benjamin wasn't home, he said he wanted to talk to me about something. For the life of me, I couldn't understand why. So I asked him if anything was wrong. He said he was very upset and uncomfortable about the fact that Benjamin was gay. You could have knocked me over with a feather! Where did he get that information? He said they had talked a few days earlier and he had asked our son if he had a girlfriend, to which he replied, "No, but I have a boyfriend." This freaked the roomie out and he asked for a room change immediately, but the school said they had to wait the full six weeks it required before they would make the change.

The young man said he had made a few calls and had found another gay guy on their hall and had asked him if he would swap roommates with him. Apparently, he had no plans of spending any nights in the same room with our son. Stunned, I called the school to ask if they might make an exception to the rules so Benjamin would have somewhere to sleep, but was unsuccessful. After he returned from his errands, I questioned him about it, and he said he did indeed have a boyfriend and had told his roommate that he was gay. Why would he do such a thing? Didn't he know this bit of information might not be well received?

Such information was too much for me, and I tried not to think about it. I knew he had definitely made life difficult for himself for the next six weeks.

The big day arrived. We were up at 5:45 and braced ourselves for the day, which was supposed to be fun and exciting but turned into the day from the pit of you know where. Benjamin was so nervous he threw up several times. Finally, he settled down and we were on the road by 7:00. The trip went smooth, and we were very excited to find out the dorm he was in had elevators!

We arrived before the loving and kind roommate and had Benjamin set up in no time. So we went to get books, a parking pass, and other necessary things. We returned to his room after lunch to find the roommate and his parents there unpacking. They had changed everything around to suit their little darling and rolled up Benjamin's new rug and stuck it in the corner. Under my breath I said, "Who are these people? Are they royalty?" Their son was obviously spoiled to the bone and had a mega fridge, microwave with a toaster for bagels, which by the way, was contraband, and a super nice television and sound system. We exchanged formalities and left.

Benjamin walked out to the van with us and seemed more relaxed than I thought he would be. He was ready for us to leave. I managed not to cry, and we hugged and kissed good-bye. I told him I loved him and to call if he needed anything. We turned to leave and heard someone blow their car horn. We turned back around quickly, just in time to see Benjamin standing in the path of an SUV. Thankfully, the driver had lightning reflexes and he was unharmed. The poor kid looked embarrassed and I said a little prayer for God to protect him in our absence and we left.

After we returned home from the great exodus I felt like I had aged ten years. It had indeed been a taxing day. Our son was on his own, no mom or dad to tell him what to do. Our job was done; we had raised him in the "nurture and admonition of the Lord," taught him Bible verses, loved him, encouraged him, and tried to teach him how he should live. He had the Word hidden in his heart and every once in a while, a verse would pop out of his mouth. I knew the Lord would use those verses hidden deep within him and would bring them back to his mind when he needed them. He will be surprised when that happens, and I hope he will be glad they are there.

The Lord can use things learned in childhood that we might not even remember learning, and Satan can't steal the Word that is hidden in our hearts. My prayer for Benjamin is that those verses learned in childhood will bring peace and rest to my son's soul. All I want for him is happiness, contentment, and peace with his past. I am trusting God to send Benjamin a Christian friend who will love him as Jesus does, and for God to reveal truth and expose lies.

I had a lot of time to think about the past two years in Benjamin's absence. With him away, I felt like I had more freedom to meditate on what we had experienced and pray for wisdom and understanding for the future events that might take place. One particular comment Benjamin had made disturbed me, the thought of him asking God to take his same-sex feelings away and him not doing it circled around my brain. The very thought has haunted me since the first time I heard it. Why, indeed, would God not answer a child's prayer? It finally occurred to me, that if we want to rid our minds of sinful or bad thoughts, we have to replace them with something good and right, just as the speaker said at the Minister of Education conference. The Word says to think on good things.

> Finally, brothers (or sisters), whatever is true, whatever is noble, whatever is right, whatever is pure, whatever is lovely, whatever is admirable-if anything is excellent or praiseworthy-think about such things. Whatever you have learned or received or heard from me, or seen in me-put it into practice. And the God of peace will be with you. Philippians 4:8,9 (NIV)

Peter also admonishes us to guard our minds. I believe the battle with sin is won or lost in the mind. If we feed our brains with sinful material, we will be sinful. If we feed our brains with scripture and time spent in prayer, we have a better chance of winning the battle. Remember the old saying, "you are what you eat"? That applies to our spiritual and emotional being as well as physical.

> Wherefore gird up the loins of your mind, be sober, and hope to the end for the grace that is to be brought unto you at the revelation of Jesus Christ; As obedient children, not fashioning yourselves according to the former lusts in your ignorance: But as he which has called you is holy, so be ye holy in all manner of conversation; Because it is written, Be ye holy; for I am holy. I Peter 1:13–16 (KJV)

These verses were not new to me. I remembered them from studying God's word for over twenty-five years.

Since Benjamin was just a child at the time of his abuse, he did not know these things and had no knowledge of the importance of filtering the thoughts that came into his mind. Because of the emotional and physical trauma, thoughts of the abuse surely filled his thought-life continually and were probably followed by thoughts of guilt and shame, feelings he didn't understand and had no former reference of. As he grew older and having had continual thoughts of the abuse and then later viewing pornography, it fueled the desire for the feelings he had. It would prove nearly impossible for God to take the feelings away while he at the same time was feeding his mind with such material. You have to replace the bad with good.

I feel confident that immediate counseling was needed and would have proven invaluable to his healing and am deeply saddened he did not get it. I can't help but wonder how our lives would be now had we known the truth about the abuse earlier.

I don't know the answer to these things, but I do know that God can take something broken and make it whole again and the latter will excel the former. As Jeremiah tells us in Jeremiah 18:3,4

> So I went down to the potter's house, and I saw him working at the wheel. But the pot he was shaping from the clay was marred in his hands; so the potter formed it into another pot, shaping it as seemed best to him. Jeremiah 18:3,4 (NIV)

God can take Benjamin's brokenness and shape it into something that is best to him. As God's children, he can take things that happen to us that may or may not be his perfect will for us and use them for good. Because we live in a sin-cursed world inhabited by sinful people, many inflict pain or suffering on others. But God can take something so evil and despicable as sexual abuse and, like the potter and the clay, take the brokenness of the vessel and make it into something beautiful and valuable for his use. I must believe that God has a plan for my son that will bring glory to him and for the good of others. It is my fervent prayer.

The next month and a half proved uneventful. Benjamin rarely came home on the weekend and didn't call. If we wanted to talk to him, we had to call. Everything was going great he said.

The time for our church ladies' annual retreat at Callaway Gardens arrived in late September. As you recall earlier in the book, the retreat of the previous year was very emotional. This year would be different; I felt like a bird from prison. I no longer had to drag my crying towel along with me. Since Benjamin was now in college, there was a liberated feeling in my soul. I intended to hear every word God had for me and knew I would be blessed tremendously! All of us ladies were worked up big time and could barely wait to go. It always proves to be a time of encouragement and blessing, and it gives us the chance to get better acquainted with our sisters in Christ.

Once we arrived at the conference and had our dinner, we headed out for the evening session. What an awesome time! It seemed that each speaker had been instructed to bring a word especially to me. At the end of the session, there was praise and worship and hundreds gathered at the front of the room in prayer; how God moved! I didn't want it to end, but there would be more sessions tomorrow, and I couldn't wait to see what God would say to me. After the session, we headed back to the villa for a precious and sweet time in prayer with our sisters and had a restful night's sleep.

The following day proved to outdo the evening before. God was indeed present among us, and each of us was sad to see the conference come to an end. I had a ball, considering the only underwear I had for the trip was on my body. Who forgets to pack underwear? Evidently, I was so excited about the conference, I wasn't thinking about anything else! Thank the Lord it was only a two day trip. We returned in time for the Sunday evening service. After the service was over, one of the girls who went on the trip came to me and asked how Benjamin was doing. I said fine; she then said that she was praying for me, and she didn't know how I could smile and keep going day after day. It was obvious she knew Benjamin's secret, but how did she know? She proceeded to tell me how she had seen him at a high school football game holding hands with his "friend."

I briefly thought of suicide, but I had come too far for that. She said I was an inspiration to her, and for the life of me, I couldn't figure out why. We talked a long time until someone finally turned the lights out, signaling that we should get a life and go home. We hugged and departed. I was deeply touched and encouraged by her sincere concern. It blessed my heart to know there were people praying for me I didn't even know about.

Now about the underwear, or the absence thereof, I was later presented with a large picture frame with a huge pair of ugly underwear neatly pressed inside that said, "In case of emergency, break glass."

Don't you just love these girls!

The Journey

....

Isn't it convenient how we categorize sin? Human beings think that we can put our sins in categories according to their sinfulness. Little sins are things like lying, cheating on our taxes, gossiping often disguised as a prayer request, and keeping too much change the cashier gave us by mistake that she will probably have to ante up at quitting time.

Then there are the middle-of-the road type sins like adultery, embezzlement, and backsliding—returning to our old lifestyle before Christ came into our heart. The biggies are murder, torturing small animals or children, and to some people, living the homosexual lifestyle.

We can commit small infractions, because after all, everybody tells a little white lie every once in a while. We can commit adultery because "my husband just doesn't understand me and he snores too loud." Even murder can be justified; "He abused me verbally and physically, wouldn't give me any money and made me do horrible things, like have his dinner on the table at exactly 5:00, and if I didn't, he would slap me around and make me rub his feet afterwards."

But some believe that homosexuality is the ultimate sin. Someone who commits such acts is "sick in the head and will burn in hell; if they would get saved, accept Christ into their heart, they wouldn't do such disgusting and perverse things." How can we say such things? May God have mercy on us. Christians can be cold and judgmental. Who gave us the authority to pass judgment on others? Why is it that other people's sins are always worse than ours? Jesus had plenty to say about that.

> Do not judge, or you too will be judged. For in the same way you judge others, you will be judged, and with the measure you use, it will be measured to you. Why do you look at the speck of sawdust in your brother's eye and pay no attention to the plank in your own eye? How can you say to your brother, 'Let me take the speck out of your eye,' when all the time there is a plank in your own eye? You hypocrite, first take the plank out of your own eye, and then you will see clearly to remove the speck from your bother's eye. Matthew 7:1–5(NIV)

These things ought not be.

In the early years of my conversion, I too had a plank in my eye. Not only did I judge other's motives and actions, I was quick to pass judgment on their words and deeds. The more I matured in my Christian walk, the more I realized God was not pleased with such cruel comments and attitudes. Guilt plagued me when I blasted harsh words. I also condemned the homosexual movement and had the same opinion as I mentioned before: "if they would get saved, they wouldn't do such things." I didn't do such things and therefore I was better than they.

Every time I thought I had my mouth under control, I would lash out at someone or something and feel ashamed and embarrassed before God. Early in our marriage, I often prayed for patience, and it seemed like around that time, a trial came along. I was very young in the faith and didn't know that God's word says in Romans 5:3 (KJV), "And not only so, but we glory in tribulations also: knowing that tribulation worketh patience." James 1:3 (KJV) also confirms this fact; "Knowing this, that the trying of your faith worketh patience." On one such occasion, my husband asked if I was praying for patience again, and I said yes. His anxious reply was, "No wonder all this is happening! Can't you pray about something else?" But asking God to help me was my only resolve. I wanted desperately to change and be more kind and understanding.

I finally got my prayer answered, but not before I experienced something I had mocked and ridiculed. I am not saying that my child experienced sexual abuse to teach me humility, but I am saying God used that terrible trial to teach me a valuable lesson. There is nothing that will knock the pride out of you like having your child tell you that he is gay. My arrogance received a slap in the face, and suddenly I realized I was not the perfect person I thought I was. My pride and assurance of my abilities as a parent were stripped away in a single sweep of God's hand. The only thing I could do was cry out to God from my knees and beg for mercy and forgiveness, which he gave.

It has definitely been a journey that has taught me many truths for which I am grateful.

One being, our righteousness is like filthy rags (Isaiah 64:6 KJV). Unworthy and undeserving are we. God blesses us because he wants to, not because we deserve it. Surely God looks down from heaven and shakes his righteous head, saying, "Will she ever learn?" We are indeed wretched and despicable, and that's on our good days.

Because God is righteous, sovereign, powerful, and holy, he owes us no explanation of his actions. He knows what we need to mold us into the likeness of his Son. Willingly, his hands can mold us, or we can be broken (like I was), and like the pot on the wheel in Jeremiah 18. We are like clay in the hand of the Master Potter, and he desires something better for us.

Through the experience with our son, I have learned many lessons, and God has brought about many changes in my life, and I am still learning. The trial we have endured has taught me to be careful with my words. In a moment's time, a person's heart can be wounded by words. Every day of my life I have to pray for God to help me weigh my words before speaking, and every day I have to go to him ashamed and embarrassed and ask forgiveness for a careless comment spoken too quickly. I've also learned that as Christians, we have to be so careful not to judge others; pride creeps in and before we know it, we have convinced ourselves that we are "more godly" because we don't do this or the other. Only God can know a person's heart and motives—we can't. I also know that there are many people around us who are hurting. Since learning of Benjamin's abuse and subsequent desire to live a gay lifestyle, I have found out there are many, many other parents, sisters, brothers, and assorted family members touched by this heartbreaking experience. Having heard unfeeling comments about "fags, queers, or sickos deserving hell," my heart has been broken for my sisters and brothers in Christ. I know how they feel.

Oh that God would give us tender hearts to reach out to those around us, offering love and compassion, including those who live an alternative lifestyle. How can we help them understand that God loves them and Christ died for them if we spew hateful words about or to them? Jesus sat with sinners on many occasions, yet he never condemned; he simply let them know that there was hope, healing, and a better way through the ultimate sacrifice he was willing to pay. We are to live our lives the way he instructs us. He is our example. We are to put our prejudices aside and reach out to those around us with the life-changing truth of the gospel.

The men and women living a gay, lesbian, bisexual, or any other lifestyle need Jesus, just like any other person on the planet. Indeed, the gay and lesbian communities are an untouched mission field. If these precious people accept Christ as their Savior, their sexual desires still may not change. Sometimes, there are deep, dark emotional scars from many different kinds of abuse a person may not be able to admit to or be willing to talk about. Their secrets may die with them. My hope and desire is to help other parents or those dealing with the pain and grief felt regarding their loved one. If I can do or say anything to help them make it through the dark, dark valley, I count myself blessed by the opportunity.

I have experienced many dark and devastating days and many nights when I didn't want to go to bed because I knew there would be nightmares. But God has brought me through great sorrow and has been my source of strength and courage when no one else was. Psalm 23 KJV has been and still is especially dear to me. Listen to what the psalmist said.

> The Lord is my shepherd; I shall not want. He maketh me to lie down in green pastures: he leadeth me beside the still waters. He restoreth my soul: he leadeth me in the paths of righteousness for his name's sake. Yea, though I walk through the valley of the shadow of death, I will fear no evil: for thou art with me; thy rod and thy staff they comfort me.

Thou preparest a table before me in the presence of
mine enemies: thou anointest my head with oil; my
cup runneth over. Surely goodness and mercy shall
follow me all the days of my life: and I will dwell in
the house of the Lord for ever. Psalm 23 (KJV)

God is my constant. When the tempestuous, violent
waves of this life seem certain to overcome me and pull
me under, God says, "Come with me, I will give you green
pastures to lie down in and beautiful, still waters to walk
beside; do not fear, for I will walk with you and restore your
soul." What precious promises we have from God's word!

Although, at times, the tears still come, yet not as often.
They flow unbidden, like torrents of rain, and I'm unable to
harness the grief. My heart and soul are poured out as an
offering to God through my many tears. The father of lies
whispers that it's my fault that my sweet son was abused; he
says my pride gave me a false sense of security, and I let my
guard down, thus allowing him to enter our home.

He says to end it all, so I won't feel the pain anymore,
but Satan is the deceiver, a liar, and the father of all lies
and seeks only to kill, steal, and destroy. Christ has come
so that I might have life, and to have it more abundantly
(John 10:10 KJV).

In life's trials, sometimes the outcome isn't as important as what happens to the person in the process of going
through the trial. It's not so much the journey of life, but how
we view the events we encounter on our way. Somewhere in
the middle of all the stuff of life we become a different person. The person that God is shaping us to be—one more
dependent on him and less dependent on self; not what I
want, but what Jesus wants for me. If we are willing, he will

also teach us things like undying faith, unconditional love, unending trust, and everlasting peace.

I have learned that a season of grief encourages a person to reevaluate their priorities, to put things in proper perspective and not get caught up in the little irritations of life. There are many other things that warrant our attention which are vital to mankind's existence, like encouraging and loving others with an unconditional love like the Savior did, validating someone's concerns no matter how trivial they may seem to us, meeting the basic needs of those around us when we have the means to do so, and showing compassion to the suffering.

If you ask me if my son has renounced the gay lifestyle and is serving Jesus with all of his heart and soul, I will have to say no. But I have many precious promises from God's Word that encourage me daily.

> This is what the Lord says, he who made the earth, the Lord who formed it and established it-the Lord is his name. "Call to me and I will answer you and tell you great and unsearchable things you do not know." Jeremiah 33:2,3 (NIV)

Isaiah tells us in chapter 43:18,19 (NIV); "Forget the former things; do not dwell on the past. See, I am doing a new thing! Now it springs up; do you not perceive it? I am making a way in the desert and streams in the wasteland."

From Isaiah, I know my son can be rescued from his captivity and set free.

> Can plunder be taken from warriors, or captives rescued from the fierce? But this is what the Lord says: "Yes, captives will be taken from warriors, and plunder retrieved from the fierce; I will contend

with those who contend with you, and your children I will save." Isaiah 49:24,25 (NIV)

What greater promise is there?

There is No Place Like Home

At the beginning of this book, I likened myself to Dorothy in *The Wizard of Oz*. I was in a terrible storm and didn't know if I would ever emerge from it. I was beaten about and felt fairly certain I would not come out alive—and wasn't sure I wanted to. If I did make it out alive, I would probably find myself in a place I had never been before; somewhere strange with red, purple, and yellow horses and munchkins and flying monkeys. A place where the Good Witch Glinda urged me to follow the yellow brick road to the Emerald City so the Wizard could help me get back home.

Only, around every turn, I was met with resistance; fear, doubt, and anger seized my soul, and I felt so alone.

On my journey, I met and became like the Scarecrow with no brain. I thought I was losing my mind, a Tin Man without a heart; mine was broken, and a Timid Lion with no courage; I was filled with fear. We four joined forces and forged on to the Emerald City so we each could be granted our wish from the Wizard.

On and on the yellow brick road went, winding around rude, talking apple trees, attacks by the Wicked Witch of the West, and a spell-laden poppy field that caused us to fall into a deep sleep, only to be thankfully awakened by a freak snowstorm courtesy of that Good Witch Glinda.

Against all odds, we made it to the Emerald City and were welcomed with singing, "You're out of the woods, you're out of the dark, you're out of the night, step into the sun, step into the light."

Without realizing it, I had indeed stepped out of the dark night of my weary soul and stepped into the light, the Son's light that sustained me through my long, trying journey. Along with the Scarecrow, the Tin Man, and the Timid Lion, I have received what I asked for, though not from the Wizard.

You see, there was no real Wizard, just a round, little man with smoke and mirrors, hiding behind a curtain. When Dorothy and the trio first arrived at the Emerald City and asked the Wizard to grant their requests, he sent them on a ridiculous mission to steal the broom of the Wicked Witch of the West, hoping they would not return because he knew he was unable to grant things he could not see or hold in his hand.

To his amazement, Dorothy and the trio did return with the broomstick, although in the process, Dorothy and Toto were captured and held prisoner by the Wicked Witch. By some miracle, the Tin Man had developed a love for Dorothy and Toto and was determined to rescue them from the Wicked Witch of the West. Unbelievably, the Scarecrow intelligently planned a means of attack so they could rescue Dorothy, and the Lion bravely marched on with his newfound courage. They didn't realize it, but the very things they had asked the Wizard for were miraculously provided, not by the Wizard, but by a higher power.

So it is with me. God has not given me "the spirit of fear, but of power, and of love, and of a sound mind" (2 Timothy 1:7 KJV). God's grace proved sufficient for me during my trial. When I felt like I could not go on, the

Lord granted me courage for the journey. I could not have made it otherwise.

I am forever grateful.

Benjamin is on his way down that yellow brick road too. He ran away from what he knew to be true and ventured on a journey far, far from home. On his journey, he has encountered lions, tigers, and bears—oh my! Lions that want to steal his courage to find his way back, tigers that want him to remain a prisoner of his mind, and bears that want to tear his heart to shreds so he won't feel anything. But God, "will with the temptation also make a way to escape, that ye may be able to bear it" (1 Corinthians 10:13b KJV).

God the Father has equipped Benjamin, and all who know Jesus as Savior, with "ruby slippers," the crimson blood of Jesus Christ that was shed for his sin to bring him back into fellowship with God the Father, and Jesus, his Son.

When Glinda the Good Witch placed the ruby slippers on Dorothy's feet, she unknowingly received the power to return home at any time simply by tapping them together three times and saying, "There's no place like home." It never crossed Dorothy's mind that the ruby slippers were crucial for her return home. The unbelievable power the slippers possessed was for Dorothy and she alone, but she didn't realize it until the Wicked Witch of the West tried to remove them from her feet. An unknown force gave the Wicked Witch the shock of her life, and even Dorothy couldn't remove them, even though she desperately tried in order to save Toto.

Like Dorothy, who had no idea the ruby slippers Glinda had placed on her feet had the power to take her home to

Auntie Em at any time, so Benjamin has forgotten that the blood of Jesus can heal all wounds and draw him back into the Father's outstretched arms. Because Benjamin asked Jesus into his heart as a child, he has assurance of his salvation and a home in heaven some day. Like the ruby slippers, the precious blood of Jesus applied to Benjamin's heart can never be removed, regardless of his actions. It is there to stay.

Forgiveness and restoration are made possible by the precious blood of the Savior. It has the power to bring Benjamin home at any time if he will ask him. It has been there all along.

There is no place like home.

Epilogue

....

Mother Eve came to me in a dream and said, "Deny your wayward heart, my daughter, deny your wayward heart. The heart is deceitful above all things, and desperately wicked: who can know it?" (Jeremiah 17:9 KJV). Curious and confused, I looked deeply into her sad eyes; her sorrow and shame illuminated through the windows of her soul. "God bestowed on me the honor of giving birth to humanity. How He loved and trusted me! Was I worthy of His trust? No, in return I rebelled and disobeyed the only command He issued. In a fleeting moment of time, I plunged the entire human race into a sea of sin. It has been so ever since.

"Down through the ages of time it has remained. From birth, man struggles helplessly against the waves that attempt to consume him. Many times, he nearly drowns in the angry, treacherous sea of sin. The waves pull him under over and over, deeper, deeper. Time and again, someone, somewhere reaches down and pulls him up just before it is too late. Miraculously, his breath is restored and he finds himself resting on the shore. Sadly, he will soon return to the awful, ravenous sea, not knowing if he will succumb to its angry waves this time or if he will survive. You are no exception, dear daughter. The heart is deceitful above all things, and desperately wicked: who can know it?" (Jeremiah 17:9 KJV).

But if I can't know my own heart, what will become of

me? Will I drown in the sea of sin? How can I learn what is in my heart? Who will show me? "There is one who can reveal your heart to you. He is able to expose the lies, the bitterness and the rebellion that is secretly hidden away in the darkest corners of your heart. You must be willing to give Him your heart, even though you may be ashamed for Him to see what is inside.

"Because of my rebellion, God sent his Son as a sacrifice for the sin of man. He knew we would need a Redeemer, a Savior who could take the punishment we deserved so we could be forgiven. He knew from the beginning I would sin in the Garden, he even knew before Adam was created that I would be deceived. God could have prevented my willful act of disobedience, but he longed for me to love and obey him from a heart of love. He gave me a choice, and regrettably, I made the wrong choice; so be careful, my daughter.

"Say to the Father, 'Search me, O God, and know my heart; test me and know my anxious thoughts. See if there is any offensive way in me, and lead me in the way everlasting' (Psalm 139:23,24 NIV). He will reveal your heart to you. He can free you from what lies deep inside your heart; all you must do is ask."

Be prepared, my sisters, God may reveal to you as he did to me; my heart was filled with bitterness.

Bitterness is persistent and ruthless. It sends its roots down deep and rapidly grows. Soon it wraps itself around our heart, taking up so much space that there is no room for anything else. The garden of our heart quickly becomes root bound; large roots send out smaller tendrils that wrap ever tightly until the heart is choked with bitterness. There is no more room for kindness, tenderness, patience or love.

Persistently the roots continue, wrapping themselves around every area of our life, spilling criticism, anger, harsh attitudes and words onto others. The bitterness chokes even the most resilient relationships; even the ones that mean the most to us—the ones closest to our heart. But the heart is full of bitterness, not of love, and the ever-growing root springs forth and latches onto all who are near. Friends and acquaintances flee in fear—fear that the bitterness in our heart might consume theirs, fear of being entangled in the vines that shoot forth in search of its next victim.

Inevitably, we with the bitter heart are alone. The benefit of our company doesn't exceed the punishment they must endure to be near us. Such a relationship is emotionally taxing and extremely high maintenance. Those we consider a friend simply can't devote the time and effort necessary to continue the relationship. The stark realization finally becomes apparent. Not only are we completely consumed with our bitterness, but we are painfully alone. If we are honest with our self, we know the reason why. How did this happen? Can a person rid oneself of the awful condition they are in or are they destined to a life of loneliness?

A once vibrant life lived for the Lord can be vaguely recalled to memory. Once we felt joy in our heart and longed for time to spend alone with God. How sweet the fellowship was then! It seems like a lifetime has passed since we had those feelings.

Something awful happened. Something we couldn't control; something we didn't like or want, something painful like a broken marriage, a broken heart, a broken friendship. Maybe it was a disappointment, deception, or disagreement. Perhaps it was undeserved treatment or an unanswered prayer. It could be death, everyone dreads death, especially the death of a child, spouse, parent, or close friend. Maybe it was something worse than death, like physical or sexual abuse, which sometimes troubles the victim for a lifetime.

These things are hard to endure, and as long as we are in our human bodies, we will endure hardship. Job said, "man born of woman is of few days and full of trouble" (Job 14:1 NIV).

Our hardships and trials don't make us bitter; it is our response to them that does. How we respond to trials determines our attitude. We can become bitter or we can go to God in prayer and bare our soul to him and cry out for help. Our heavenly Father wants us to pour out our heart to him and tell him exactly how we feel.

The ugly, horrible details don't disturb him; his desire is to know us, even when we are angry because he knows our pain and longs to help us. He is after all, the sympathizing Savior. His heart was broken at the tomb of Lazarus and he wept openly. The rebellion of his children, Israel, broke his heart. Still it breaks over the sin that is widespread across the earth.

The Lord is near to those who have a broken heart, and he will take the pieces, if we surrender them, and make us into a new vessel that can be used by the Master. But if we want to keep certain pieces of a broken life or heart, we make it difficult for the Savior to bring healing and restoration to us. Our wholeness depends on us—we must bring every disgusting shred of evidence of a broken life to him.

We may plead with God, "Please just let me keep this one thing, I can't release it, it hurt me so much I can't possibly let it go. I have to hold on, I can't forgive. The pain and agony it caused me was so severe I could never just let it go. Some things can't be forgiven." But remember—without every piece, the potter can't create a vessel for his use. Surrender all and he will restore all.

That is easier said than done.

There was a time, not so very long ago, something terrible broke my heart, and I told God that I couldn't forgive. I didn't want to let go of my pain, but God, who is rich in mercy, gently and lovingly brought me through the pain and put all my pieces back together.

In a dream, I saw myself scurrying around, picking up all of the scattered pieces of my life and carefully putting each one inside a large box. The search went on for days. The pieces were strewn about the house; some well hidden in dark corners, under furniture, in the closet, high on a shelf. Just when I thought I had them all, I remembered the one I hold close to my heart, the one piece that I hold dear, the one that controls my thoughts and invades every part of my life. I carry it everywhere I go and never leave home without it.

My attitude and behavior are justified by this piece. No one would deny me the anger and bitterness I have come to love. I have a right to be angry. They would do the same if it were them.

The box isn't full, but I offer it to the Master anyway. With love and compassion, he stretches out his open hand to me. There is a look of sadness in his eyes as he patiently waits for surrender. Oh, how he is longsuffering and kind! Oh, how he loves me so! I can't imagine why he would want me but he still waits with his arm outstretched. From somewhere deep inside my soul I find the courage to extend my hand to touch his.

Time stands still; we are two figures standing, waiting,

unable to move. Suddenly, my mind is flooded with past hurts, bitterness, sadness, grief, and confusion. Weary from the baggage I've carried for so long, the thought of releasing the burden into God's hand brings a faint glimmer of hope.

I'm so exhausted from lugging my baggage around; could it be possible to be free from the burden I bear? My heart beats wildly as I excitedly think that I might be free. In my hand lies the final piece of my broken heart and life; it is true, I can carry it no more.

In slow motion, my fingers begin to open and my burden is exposed. Hesitantly, I place it in the Lord's hand.

The lover of my soul receives it, and a look of approval can be seen on his face. "Now my child, I will make you a vessel of honor. I'll remove your scars and repair the brokenness. The root of bitterness can no longer flourish and will soon die. In its place will bloom faith and trust rooted in love and peace and contentment."

At last, I am free. And you can be too; all we must do is ask.

Does this mean there will be no more trials? Unfortunately, as long as we live on this earth, we will experience trials and tests. But we have the promise of God that he will be with us through every test and will comfort us in all of our trials. His word is true.

> Praise be to the God and Father of our Lord Jesus Christ, the Father of compassion and the God of all comfort, who comforts us in all our troubles, so that we can comfort those in any trouble with the comfort we ourselves have received from God. 2 Corinthians 1:3,4 (NIV)

Isaiah 43:2 (NIV) tells us, "When you pass through the waters, I will be with you; and when you pass through the rivers, they will not sweep over you. When you walk through the fire, you will not be burned; the flames will not set you ablaze."

And finally, Lamentations encourages us with these words.

> I remember my affliction and my wandering, the bitterness and the gall. I well remember them, and my soul is downcast within me. Yet this I call to mind and therefore I have hope: Because of the Lord's great love we are not consumed, for his compassions never fail. They are new every morning; great is your faithfulness. I say to myself, "The Lord is my portion; therefore I will wait for him." Lamentations 3:19–24 (NIV)

Dear sister, I have a dream for you. If you are wandering around in the darkness of night, tightly gripping the "final piece of brokenness" in your hand, go ahead—surrender to the Savior, and he will give you peace in exchange for your bitterness. It doesn't matter what it is that has consumed you; he will take it and you will be free. Free from guilt, anger, and depression. Free to love, laugh, and forgive. You can be free; just ask.